SECOND REVISED AND EXPANDED EDITION

CHARLES BERLITZ

PASSPORT TO

SPANISH

A SIGNET BOOK

SIGNET
Published by the Penguin Group
Penguin Books USA Inc., 375 Hudson Street,
New York, New York 10014, U.S.A.
Penguin Books Ltd, 27 Wrights Lane,
London W8 5TZ, England
Penguin Books Australia Ltd, Ringwood,
Victoria, Australia
Penguin Books Canada Ltd, 10 Alcorn Avenue,
Toronto, Ontario, Canada M4V 3B2
Penguin Books (N.Z.) Ltd, 182–190 Wairau Road,
Auckland 10, New Zealand

Penguin Books Ltd, Registered Offices:
Harmondsworth, Middlesex, England

Published by Signet, an imprint of New American Library,
a division of Penguin Books USA Inc.

First Signet Printing, April, 1974
First Printing (Revised and Expanded Edition), March, 1986
Second Revised and Expanded Edition (Sixth Printing), August, 1993
13 12 11 10 9 8 7 6

 REGISTERED TRADEMARK—MARCA REGISTRADA

PRINTED IN THE UNITED STATES OF AMERICA

whether you are facing a restaurant menu or
    a hotel desk clerk,
Whether you are visiting a museum or stop-
    ping at a gas station,
Whether you need directions or want to strike
    up a casual conversation,
Whether you have to deal with a medical emer-
    gency or a mechanical breakdown,
Whether you want to establish trust and good
    feelings in a business meeting or demon-
    strate warmth and courtesy in personal deal-
    ings, this one book is your

PASSPORT TO SPANISH

SECOND REVISED AND EXPANDED EDITION

agua caliente

Contents

 **Preface**

Passport to Spanish is not a conventional phrasebook, but rather a basis for speaking and understanding Spanish. The short sentences contain the key words and phrases most useful for travel, business, shopping, restaurants, sightseeing and, most importantly, for communicating with the people of the Spanish-speaking world. You will be surprised and gratified by the friendly relations you establish when you take the trouble to address people in Spain and Latin America in their rich and expressive language.

This book is designed to provide easy and instant communication. The phrases are short, pertinent to situations of daily life, and grouped for easy reference, so that you can find the exact section you need at any moment.

Each phrase, designed for your trip to a Spanish-speaking area, is written first in English, then in Spanish, and finally in easy to pronounce phonetics. When a Spanish word has a syllable that must be stressed, this syllable is written in capitals. This will give an authentic tone to your accent and help the people in the country you are visiting to undertand you easily.

To facilitate mutual understanding we have added special sections to certain chapters. These are called POINT TO THE ANSWER. Here the first sentence is in Spanish with the English written below. A note in Spanish requests the person to whom you are speaking to point to the answer to your specific question.

The use of this book will more than double your enjoyment of a trip abroad and also save you money. Besides the economic factor, why visit a foreign country if you can't break the language barrier and communicate with the new and interesting people you meet? You might as well stay home and see the palaces and monuments of the country on TV. Who wants to be limited to one language when acquiring a new language can be so easy and enjoyable!

One can speak and understand current everyday Spanish with comparatively few words and phrases—perhaps 1,600 to 1,900, which is less than the number given in the dictionary at the end of this book. By using the same short phrases over and over in the various situations where they normally occur, you will acquire them without conscious effort. They will become a part of your own vocabulary and of your memory bank and that is, after all, the only secret to learning a language.

Since Spanish is descended from Latin, it shares a great deal of vocabularly with Italian, French, and Portuguese, and also with English, from the days of the Roman occupation of ancient England. You are already familiar with several thousand Spanish words differing from their English equivalents only slightly in spelling and pronunciation. See page 147 for examples. You will find that you already have an extensive vocabulary in Spanish!

⤳ How to Acquire an Instant Spanish Accent

Every word or sentence in this book is presented in English, in Spanish, and in an easy-to-read pronunciation system to help you say the Spanish correctly. Just pronounce the third line as if you were reading English. Stress the syllables printed in capital letters.

English: *Do you speak Spanish?*
Spanish: *¿Habla Usted español?*
Pronunciation: *¿AH-bla oo-STED ess-pahn-YOHL?*

Although the following points are made clear in the third line, they will be helpful for you in pronouncing and reading Spanish generally:

The vowels a, e, i, o, u are pronounced *ah, eh, ee, oh, oo,* respectively. In our pronunciation system, we have added an *h* to some syllables, such as *do* and *to,* to remind you to pronounce them *doh* and *toh* and not to confuse them with the sounds of the English words "do" and "to." (Note that *i* standing alone in the pronunciation line represents the sound of the English word "I" or "eye.")

ll is pronounced like the *lli* in *million.*

ñ is pronounced like the *ny* in *canyon.*

j is pronounced like the English *h.*

g before *e* and *i* is also pronounced like the English *h* but with a stronger and more guttural sound.

The Spanish h is silent.

The combination *ay* or *ai* is pronounced like the English word "I."

In most parts of Spain c before e or i, or z before any letter, is pronounced like the English *th* in *think,* rather like a lisp. In southern Spain and in Latin America these letters generally sound like an *s.* We have written them as *s* in the pronounciation line because this is easier to say and more widely used.

And, finally, to approximate an authentic Spanish or Latin American way of speaking, be sure to roll the r, especially the double rr.

With this advice, and the easy pronounciation reminder under each word, you are almost certain to be told: *¡Usted tiene un acento muy bueno!* ¡oo-STED T'YEH-neh oon ah-SEN-toh mwee BWEH-no! Which means: "You have a very good accent!"

1. Greetings and Introductions

When addressing people call them *Señor, Señora,* or *Señorita* with or *without* adding their last names. Even when you say simply *Buenos días* ("Good morning" or "Good day") it is more polite to add one of these titles to it.

Mr. (or) Sir	Mrs. (or) Madam	MISS
Señor	Señora	Señorita
sen-YOR	*sen-YO-ra*	*sen-yo-REE-ta*

Good morning, sir.
Buenos días, señor.
BWEH-nohs DEE-yahs,
  sen-YOR.

Good afternoon, madam.
Buenas tardes, señora.
BWEH-nahs TAR-dehs,
  sen-YO-ra.

Good evening, miss.
Buenas noches, señorita.
BWEH-nahs NO-chehs,
  sen-yo-REE-ta.

How are you?
¿Cómo está usted?
¿KO-mo ess-TA oo-STED?

Very well, thank you. And you?
Muy bien, gracias. ¿Y usted?
mwee b'yen, GRA-s'yahs. ¿ee oo-STED?

Come in.
Adelante.
ah-deh-LAHN-teh.

Sit down, please.
Siéntese, por favor.
S'YEN-teh-seh, por fa-VOR.

I am Robert Gómez.
Yo soy Roberto Gómez.
yo soy ro-BEHR-toh GO-mess.

Your name, please?
¿Su nombre, por favor?
¿soo NOHM-breh, por fa-VOR?

May I introduce . . .
Le presento a . . .
leh preh-SEN-toh ah . . .

Very happy to meet you.
Mucho gusto.
MOO-cho GOO-sto.

1

The pleasure is mine.
El gusto es mío.
el GOO-sto ess MEE-yo.

What country are you from?
¿De qué país es Ud.?
deh keh pa-EESS ess oo-STED?

I am from the United States.
Yo soy de los Estados Unidos.
yo soy deh lohs ess-TA-dohs oo-NEE-dohs.

What city are you from?
¿De qué ciudad es Ud.?
deh keh s'yoo-DAHD ess oo-STED?

Enjoy your visit!
¡Que goce de su visita!
keh GO-seh deh soo vee-SEE-ta!

Very kind (of you).
Muy amable.
mwee ah-MA-bleh.

Goodbye.
Adiós.
ah-D'YOHS.

So long.
Hasta luego.
AH-sta LWEH-go.

Until we meet again.
Hasta la vista.
AH-sta la VEE-sta.

A propósito (By the way): The word for "you"—**usted**— is almost always written in the abbreviated form **Ud.** or **Vd.** In future sections we will write in this way since this is how you will see it.

2. Basic Expressions

Learn the following expressions by heart. You will use them every time you speak Spanish to someone. If you memorize these expressions and the numbers in the next section you will find that you can ask prices, directions, and generally make your wishes known.

Yes.	**No.**	**Perhaps.**	**Of course.**
Sí.	No.	Quizá.	Por supuesto.
see.	*no.*	*kee-SA.*	*por soo-PWESS-toh.*

Please.	**Thank you.**	**You are welcome.**
Por favor.	Gracias.	De nada.
por fa-VOR.	*GRA-s'yahs.*	*deh NA-da.*

Pardon.	**I'm sorry.**	**It's all right.**
Perdón.	Lo siento.	Está bien.
pehr-DOHN.	*lo S'YEN-toh.*	*ess-TA b'yen.*

Here.	**There.**	**This.**	**That.**
Aquí.	Allí.	Esto.	Eso.
ah-KEE.	*ahl-YEE.*	*ESS-toh.*	*ES-so.*

Do you speak English?	**I speak Spanish a little.**
¿Habla Ud. inglés?	Hablo español un poco.
¿AH-bla oo-STED een-GLEHS?	*AH-blo ess-pahn-YOHL oon PO-ko.*

Do you understand?	**I understand.**
¿Comprende Ud.?	Yo comprendo.
¿kom-PREN-deh oo-STED?	*yo kom-PREN-doh.*

I don't understand.	**Very well.**
Yo no comprendo.	Muy bien.
yo no kom-PREN-doh.	*mwee b'yen.*

When?
¿Cuándo?
¿KWAHN-doh?

How far?
¿A qué distancia?
¿ah keh dees-TANH-s'ya?

How much time?
¿Cuánto tiempo?
¿KWAHN-toh T'YEM-po?

How?
¿Cómo?
¿KO-mo?

Why not?
¿Cómo no?
¿KO-mo no?

Like this.
Así.
ah-SEE.

Not like that.
Así no.
ah-SEE no.

It is possible.
Es posible.
ess po-SEE-bleh.

It is not possible.
No es posible.
no ess po-SEE-bleh.

Now.
Ahora.
ah-OH-ra.

Not now.
Ahora no.
ah-OH-ra no.

Later.
Más tarde.
mahs TAR-deh.

That's fine.
Está bien.
ess-TA-b'yen.

It's very good.
Es muy bueno.
ess mwee BWEH-no.

It's not good.
No es bueno.
no ess BWEH-no.

It doesn't matter.
No importa.
no eem-POR-ta.

It's very important.
Es muy importante.
ess mwee eem-por-TAHN-teh.

Speak slowly, please.
Hable despacio, por favor.
AH-bleh deh-SPA-s'yo, por fa-VOR.

Repeat, please.
Repita, por favor.
reh-PEE-ta, por fa-VOR.

Write it, please.
Escríbalo, por favor.
es-KREE-ba-lo, por fa-VOR.

Who is it?
¿Quién es?
¿k'yen ess?

Come in.
Entre.
EN-treh.

Don't come in!
¡No entre!
¡no EN-treh!

Stop.	**Wait.**	**Let's go.**	**That's all.**
Pare.	Espere.	Vamos.	Eso es todo.
PA-reh.	*ess-PEH-reh.*	*VA-mohs.*	*ES-so ess TOH-doh.*

What is this?
¿Qué es esto?
¿keh ess ESS-toh?

Where is the telephone?
¿Dónde está el teléfono?
¿DOHN-deh ess-TA el teh-LEH-fo-no?

Where is the (rest) room . . .
¿Dónde está el cuarto . . .
¿DOHN-deh ess-TA el KWAHR-toh . . .

. . . for ladies?
. . . para damas?
. . . PA-ra DA-mahs?

. . . for men?
. . para caballeros?
. . . PA-ra ka-bahl-YEH-rohs?

Show me.	**How much?**	**It's too much.**
Muéstreme.	¿Cuánto?	Es demasiado.
MWEHS-treh-meh.	*¿KWAHN-toh?*	*ess deh-ma-S'YA-doh.*

Who?	**I**	**you**	**he**	**she**
¿Quién?	yo	usted	él	ella
¿k'yen?	*yo*	(Ud.) *oo-STED*	*el*	*EL-ya*

we (men)	**we** (women)	**you** (plural)
nosotros	nosotras	ustedes (Uds.)
no-SO-trohs	*no-SO-trahs*	*oo-STED-ehs*

they (men)	**they** (women)
ellos	ellas
EL-yohs	*el-yahs*

A propósito: The phrase **por favor,** which you should always use when you ask questions or make requests, can also function for "Bring me . . . ," "I want . . . ," or "I would like . . . ," etc. Simply say **Por favor** followed by the word for whatever you want, which you can find in the dictionary section.

Remember that there are separate words for "we" and "they" according to whether men or women are referred to. In the case of a mixed group the masculine is used even if there is only one man and many women.

¿No? as a question can be used to request agreement to something or to mean "Isn't it?" "Isn't this right?" "Don't you think so?"

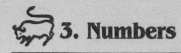# 3. Numbers

The numbers are important not only for asking prices (and perhaps to bargain) but for phone numbers, addresses, and telling time. Learn the first twenty by heart and then from 20 to 100 by tens, and you can deal with **el dinero** (money), **números de teléfono** (telephone numbers), and **direcciones** (addresses).

1	**2**	**3**	**4**
uno	dos	tres	cuatro
OO-no	*dohs*	*trehs*	*KWA-tro*

5	**6**	**7**	**8**
cinco	seis	siete	ocho
SEEN-ko	*sayss*	*S'YEH-teh*	*OH-cho*

9	**10**	**11**	**12**
nueve	diez	once	doce
N'WEH-veh	*d'yess*	*OHN-seh*	*DOH-seh*

13	**14**	**15**	**16**
trece	catorce	quince	diez y seis
TREH-seh	*ka-TOHR-seh*	*KEEN-seh*	*d'yess ee SAYSS*

17	**18**	**19**
diez y siete	diez y ocho	diez y nueve
d'yess ee S'YEH-teh	*d'yess ee OH-cho*	*d'yess ee N'WEH-veh*

20	**21**	**22**
veinte	veintiuno	veintidós
VAIN-teh	*vain-tee-OO-no*	*vain-tee-DOHS*

30	**31**	**32**
treinta	treinta y uno	treinta y dos
TRAIN-ta	*TRAIN-ta ee OO-no*	*TRAIN-ta ee dohs*

40	50	60
cuarenta	cincuenta	sesenta
kwa-REN-ta	*seen-KWEN-ta*	*seh-SEN-ta*

70	80	90
setenta	ochenta	noventa
seh-TEN-ta	*oh-CHEN-ta*	*no-VEN-ta*

100	200	300
ciento	doscientos	trescientos
S'YEN-toh	*dohs-S'YEN-tohs*	*trehs-S'YEN-tohs*

400	500	600
cuatrocientos	quinientos	seiscientos
KWA-tro-S'YEN-tohs	*keen-YEN-tohs*	*sayss-S'YEN-tohs*

700	800	900
setecientos	ochocientos	novecientos
seh-teh-S'YEN-tohs	*OH-cho-S'YEN-tohs*	*no-veh-S'YEN-tohs*

1000	1,000,000
mil	un millón
meel	*oon meel-YON*

1st	2nd	3rd
primero	segundo	tercero
pree-MEH-ro	*seh-GOON-doh*	*tehr-SEH-ro*

the last	half	zero
el último	medio	cero
el OOL-tee-mo	*MEH-d'yo*	*SEH-ro*

How much?	**How many?**	**What number?**
¿Cuánto?	¿Cuántos?	¿Qué número?
¿KWAHN-toh?	*¿KWAHN-tohs?*	*¿keh NOO-meh-ro?*

🐂 4. Arrival

Besides talking with airport officials, one of the most important things you will want to do on arrival in a Spanish-speaking country is to find your way about. For this reason we offer you here some basic "asking your way" questions and answers and call your attention to the "Point to the Answer" sections, which the people to whom you speak can use to *point out* answers to make it easier for you to understand. "Point to the Answer" sections are on pages 12, 22, 35, 42, 44, 48, 54, 58, 70, 101, 219.

Your passport, please.
Su pasaporte, por favor.
soo pa-sa-POR-teh, por fa-VOR.

I am on a visit.
Estoy de visita.
ess-TOY deh vee-SEE-ta.

For three weeks.
Por tres semanas.
por trehs seh-MA-nahs.

I am on a business trip.
Estoy en un viaje de negocios.
ess-TOY en oon V'YA-heh deh neh-GO-s'yohs.

Where is the customs?
¿Dónde está la aduana?
¿DOHN-deh ess-TA la ah-DWA-na?

Where is the baggage?
¿Dónde está el equipaje?
¿DOHN-deh ess-TA el eh-kee-PA-heh?

From flight 405?
¿Del vuelo cuatrocientos cinco?
del VWEH-lo kwa-tro-s'YEN-tohs SEEN-ko?

My bags are over there.
Mis maletas están allí.
mees ma-LEH-tahs ess-TAN ahl-YEE.

Those over there.
Aquéllas.
ah-KEL-yahs.

9

This one is mine.
Ésta es mía.
ESS-ta es MEE-ya.

That one.
Ésa.
ESS-ah.

Those bags there.
Aquellas maletas.
ah-KEL-yahs ma-LEH-tahs.

Shall I open it?
¿La abro?
¿la AH-bro?

Open it.
Ábrala.
AH-bra-la.

One moment, please.
Un momento, por favor.
oon mo-MEN-toh, por fa-VOR.

There you are.
Ya.
ya.

I have nothing to declare.
No tengo nada que declarar.
no TEN-go NA-da keh deh-kla-RAR.

This is for my personal use.
Esto es para mi uso personal.
ESS-toh ess PA-ra me OO-so pehr-so-NAHL.

This has been used.
Esto ha sido usado.
ESS-toh ah SEE-doh oo-SA-doh.

These are gifts.
Éstos son regalos.
ESS-tohs sohn reh-GA-lohs.

Where is a telephone?
¿Dónde hay un teléfono?
¿DOHN-deh I oon teh-LEH-fo-no?

Where is the bus to the city?
¿Dónde está el autobús para la ciudad?
¿DOHN-deh ess-TA el ow-toh-BOOS PA-ra la s'yoo-DAHD?

Where is the rest room?
¿Dónde está el excusado?
¿DOHN-deh ess-TA el ess-koo-SA-doh?

Where is a restaurant?
¿Dónde hay un restaurante?
¿DOHN-deh I oon rest-ow-RAHN-teh?

Porter!
¡Maletero!
¡ma-leh-TEH-ro!

Take these to a taxi.
Lleve éstas a un taxi.
L'YEH-veh ESS-tahs ah oon TAHK-see.

Taxi! Are you free?
¡Taxi! ¿Está libre?
¡TAHK-see! cess-TAH LEE-breh?

How much is it?
¿Cuánto es?
¡KWAHN-toh ess?

To the Hotel Liberty.
Al hotel Libertad.
ahl o-TEL lee-ber-TAHD.

Pardon, how can I go . . .
¿Perdón, como puedo ir . . .
¿pehr-dohn, KO-mo PWEH-doh eer . . .

. . . to the Hotel Colón?
. . . al hotel Colón?
. . . ahl o-TEL ko-LOHN?

. . . to a good restaurant?
. . . a un buen restaurante?
. . . ah oon bwehn rest-ow-RAHN-teh?

. . . to the post office?
. . . al correo?
. . . ahl ko-REH-oh?

. . . to the movies?
. . . al cine?
. . . ahl SEE-neh?

. . . to a pharmacy?
. . . a una farmacia?
. . . ah OO-na far-MA-s'ya?

. . . to a hospital?
. . . al hospital?
. . . ahl ohs-pee-TAHL?

. . . to the American consulate?
. . . al consulado americano?
. . . ahl kohn-soo-LA-doh a-meh-ree-KA-no?

British	**Canadian**	**Australian**
británico	canadiense	australiano
bree-TA-nee-ko	*ka-na-D'YEN-seh*	*owss-trahl-YA-no*

. . . to a department store? . . . to a market?
. . . a una tienda de   . . . a un mercado?
  departamentos?   . . . *ah oon mer-KA-doh?*
. . *ah OO-na t'YEN-da deh*
deh-par-ta-MEN-tohs.*

. . . to the address written here?
. . . a la dirección escrita aquí?
. . . *ah la dee-rek-S'YOHN ess-KREE-ta ah-KEE?*

Thank you very much.   **You are very kind.**
Muchas gracias.   Ud. es muy amable.
MOO-chas GRA-s'yahs.   *oo-STED ess mwee ah-MA-*
                                   bleh.

POINT TO THE ANSWER

To make sure you understand the answer to a question
you have asked, show the following section to a Spanish
speaking person so that he or she can select the answer.
The sentence in Spanish after the arrow asks the other
person to point out the answer.

 Tenga la bondad de indicar aquí abajo su con-
testación a mi pregunta. Muchísimas gracias.

Es por allí.   **En la avenida _____.**
It's that way.   On _____ Avenue.

Siga esta calle   **por do (tres) (cuatro)**
Follow this street   **calles.**
                                  for 2, (3) (4) streets.

Doble a la iz-   **Doble a la**   **Siga derecho.**
  quierda.   **derecha.**   Go straight ahead.
Turn left   Turn right.

Está cerca.   **Se puede caminar.**
It's near.   One can walk.

Está lejos.   **Se necesita un taxi.**
It's far.   One needs a taxi.

Tome el autobús   **en la esquina.**
Take the bus   on the corner.

Baje en _____
Get off at _____

A propósito: When you speak to a stranger don't forget to
say **Perdón, señor** (or **señora**) before you ask a question. If
you speak to a policeman, you can call him **señor** too.

5. Hotel—Laundry— Dry Cleaning

Although the staffs of the larger hotels have some training in English, you will find that the use of Spanish makes for better understanding and better relations, especially with the service personnel. Besides, it is fun, and you should practice Spanish at every opportunity. We have included laundry and dry cleaning in this section as these are things about which you have to make yourself understood in speaking to the hotel chambermaid or valet.

Can you recommend a good hotel?
¿Puede recomendar un buen hotel?
¿PWEH-deh reh-ko-men-DAR oon bwehn oh-TEL?

. . . a guest house?
. . . una casa de huéspedes?
. . . OO-na KA-sa deh WEHS-peh-dess?

In the center of town.
En el centro de la ciudad.
en el SEN-tro de la s'yoo-DAHD.

Not too expensive.
No muy caro.
no mwee KA-ro.

I have a reservation.
Tengo una reservación.
TEN-go OO-na reh-sehr-va-S'YOHN.

My name is ____.
Mi nombre es ____.
mee NOHM-breh ess ____.

Have you a room?
¿Tiene una habitación?
¿T'YEH-neh OO-na ah-bee-ta-S'YOHN?

I would like a room . . .
Me gustaría una habitación . . .
meh goo-sta-REE-ya OO-na ah-bee-ta-S'YOHN . . .

. . . for one person.
. . . para una persona.
. . . PA-ra OO-na pehr-SO-na.

. . . for two people.
. . . para dos personas.
. . . PA-ra dohs pehr-SO-nahs.

. . . with two beds.
. . . con dos camas.
. . . kohn dohs KA-mahs.

. . . with a bathroom.
. . . con baño.
. . . kohn BAHN-yo.

. . . with hot water.
. . . con agua caliente.
. . . kohn AH-gwa kahl-YEN-teh.

. . . air conditioned.
. . . aire acondicionado.
. . . I-reh ah-kohn-dee-s'yo-NA-doh.

. . . with a balcony.
. . . con un balcón.
. . . kohn oon bahl-KOHN.

. . . with television.
. . . con televisión.
. . . kohn teh-leh-vee-S'YOHN.

. . . with a radio
. . . con radio.
. . . *kohn RA-d'yo.*

Two connecting rooms.
Dos habitaciones contiguas.
dohs ah-bee-ta-S'YO-nehs kohn-TEE-gwahs.

How does this work?
¿Cómo funciona esto?
¿KO-mo foon-s'yo-na ESS-toh?

How much is it?   . . . per day?   . . . per week?
¿Cuánto es?   . . . por día?   . . . por semana?
¿KWAHN-toh ess? . . . por DEE-ya? . . . por seh-MA-
                                            na?

Are the meals included?
¿Están incluídas las comidas?
¿ess-TAHN een-kloo-EE-dahs lahs ko-MEE-dahs?

Is breakfast included?
¿Está incluído el desayuno?
¿ess-TA een-kloo-EE-doh el des-ah-YOO-no?

I should like to see it.
Me gustaría verla.
meh goo-sta-REE-ya VEHR-la.

Where is the bath?   . . . the shower?
¿Dónde está el baño?   . . . la ducha?
¿DOHN-deh ess-TA el   . . . la DOO-cha?
  BAHN-yo?

I want another room.   . . . higher up.
Quiero otra habitación.   . . . más arriba.
K'YEH-ro OH-tra ah-bee-   . . . mahs ah-REE-ba.
  ta-S'YOHN.

. . . better.   . . . larger.   . . . smaller.
. . . mejor.   . . . más grande.   . . . más pequeña.
. . . meh-HOR.   . . . mahs   . . . mahs peh-
                            GRAHN-deh.   KEHN-ya

I'll take this room.
Tomo esta habitación.
TOH-mo ESS-ta ah-bee-ta-S'YOHN.

I'll stay for _____ days.
Me quedaré por _____ días.
meh keh-da-REH por _____ DEE-yahs.

What time is lunch served?
¿A qué hora se sirve el almuerzo?
¿ah keh OH-ra seh SEER-veh el ahl-MWEHR-so?

What time is dinner served?
¿A qué hora se sirve la cena?
¿ah keh OH-ra seh SEER-veh la SEH-na?

I would like a bottle of mineral water and ice.
Quisiera una botella de agua mineral y hielo.
*kee-S'YEH-ra OO-na bo-TEL-ya deh AH-gwa mee-neh-
    RAHL ee YEH-lo.*

Will you send breakfast . . .
Quiere mandar el desayuno . . .
K'YEH-reh mahn-DAR el des-ah-YOO-no . . .

. . . to room number _____.
. . . a la habitación número _____.
. . ah la ah-bee-ta-S'YOHN NOO-meh-ro _____.

**Orange juice, coffee with
    (hot) milk,**
Jugo de naranja, café con
    leche,
*HOO-go deh na-RAHN-ha,
    ka-FEH kohn LEH-
    cheh,*

rolls and butter.
panecillas y mantequilla.
*pa-neh-SEEL-yahs ee
    mahn-teh-KEEL-ya.*

(For a more complete breakfast, see page 29.)

Will you send these letters?
¿Quiere mandar estas cartas?
¿K'YEH-reh mahn-DAR ESS-tahs KAR-tahs?

Will you put stamps on them?
¿Quiere ponerles estampillas?
¿K'YEH-reh po-NEHR-lehs ess-tahm-PEEL-yahs?

The key, please.
La llave, por favor.
lah L'YA-veh, por fa-VOR.

Is there any mail for me?
¿Hay correo para mí?
¿I ko-RREH-oh PA-ra mee?

Send my mail to this address.
Mande mi correo a esta dirección.
*MAHN-deh mee ko-RREH-oh ah ESS-ta
  dee-rek-S'YOHN.*

I want to speak to the manager.
Quiero hablar con el gerente.
K'YEH-ro ah-BLAR kohn el heh-REN-teh.

I need an interpreter.
Necesito un intérprete.
neh-seh-SEE-toh oon een-TEHR-preh-teh.

Are you the chambermaid?
¿Es usted la camarera?
¿ess oo-STED la ka-ma-REH-ra?

Will you change the sheets?
¿Quiere cambiar las sábanas?
¿K'YEH-reh kahm-B'YAR lahs SA-ba-nahs?

I need a blanket.   . . . a pillow.
Necesito una frazada.   . . . una almohada.
neh-seh-SEE-toh OO-na   . . . OO-na ahl-mo-AH-da.
  fra-SA-da.

... a towel. ... soap. ... toilet paper.
... una toalla. ... jabón. ... papel
... *OO-na toh-* ... *ha-BOHN.* higiénico.
 AHL-ya. ... *pa-PEL ee-*
   H'YEH-nee-ko.

This is to be cleaned.
Esto es para limpiar.
ESS-toh ess PA-ra leem-
 P'YAR.

This is to be pressed.
Esto es para planchar.
Ess-toh ess PA-ra plahn-
 CHAR.

This is to be washed.
Esto es para lavar.
ESS-toh ess PA-ra la-VAR.

This is to be repaired.
Esto es para reparar.
ESS-toh ess PA-ra reh-pa-
 RAR.

For this evening?
¿Para esta noche?
¿PA-ra ESS-ta NO-cheh?

... tomorrow?
... mañana?
... *mahn-YA-na?*

... tomorrow afternoon?
... mañana por la tarde?
... *mahn-YA-na por la*
 TAR-deh?

... tomorrow evening?
... mañana por la noche?
... *mahn-YA-na por la*
 NO-cheh?

When?
¿Cuándo?
¿KWAHN-doh?

For sure?
¿Seguro?
¿seh-GOO-ro?

Be careful with this.
Tenga cuidado con esto.
TEN-ga kwee-DA-doh kohn ESS-toh.

Don't press this with a hot iron.
No planche esto con plancha caliente.
no PLAHN-cheh ESS-toh kohn PLAHN-cha ka-L'YEN-
teh.

The dry cleaner.
La tintorería.
la teen-toh-reh-REE-ya.

Are my clothes ready?
¿Está lista mi ropa?
¿ess-TA LEES-ta mee
 RRO-pa?

When is checkout time?
¿A qué hora tenemos que dejar el cuarto?
¿Ah keh OH-ra teh-NEH-mohs keh deh-HAR el kwar-toh?

I'm leaving tomorrow morning.
Salgo mañana por la mañana.
SAHL-go mahn-YA-na por la mahn-YA-na.

Will you call me at 7 o'clock?
¿Quiere llamarme a las siete?
¿K'YEH-reh l'ya-MAR-meh ah lahs S'YEH-teh?

It's very important.	**The bill, please**
Es muy importante.	La cuenta, por favor.
ess mwee eem-por-TAHN-teh.	*la KWEN-ta, por fa-VOR.*

A propósito: Hotel floors are generally counted starting above the ground floor (**piso bajo**), so that the second floor is called the first, the third the second, etc.

POINT TO THE ANSWER

To make sure that you understand the answer to a question you might make to hotel employees, show them this so that they can point to an appropriate answer. The sentence in Spanish after the arrow asks them to point to the answer.

 Sírvase indicar en esta página su contestación a mi pregunta. Muchas gracias.

Hoy.	**Esta tarde.**	**Esta noche.**
Today.	This afternoon.	This evening.

Mañana.   **Temprano.**   **Tarde.**
Tomorrow.   Early.   Late.

Manaña por la mañana.   **Mañana por la tarde.**
Tomorrow morning.   Tomorrow afternoon.

Antes de la una.   **Antes de las dos,**   **tres, quatro,**
Before one   Before two,   **cinco.**
 o'clock.   three, four, five
        o'clock.

A las seis, siete, ocho, nueve, diez, once, doce.
At six, seven, eight, nine, ten, eleven, twelve o'clock.

lunes   **martes**   **miércoles**   **jueves**
Monday   Tuesday   Wednesday   Thursday

viernes   **sábado**   **domingo**
Friday   Saturday   Sunday

6. Time: Hours—Days—Months

In the "Hotel" section you noted that when making an appointment at a certain hour you simply put **a las** in front of the number, exept for "one o'clock" when you use **a la**. The following section shows you how to tell time in greater detail, including dates. You can make all sorts of arrangements with people by indicating the hour, the day, or the date, and adding the phrase **¿Está bien?**—Is that all right?

What time is it?
¿Qué hora es?
¿keh OH-ra ess?

It is one o'clock.
Es la una.
ess la OO-na.

It is six o'clock.
Son las seis.
sohn lahs sayss.

Half past six.
Las seis y media.
lahs sayss ee MEHD-ya.

A quarter past seven.
Las siete y cuarto.
lahs S'YEH-teh ee KWAHR-toh.

A quarter to eight.
Ocho menos cuarto.
OH-cho MEH-nohs KWAHR-toh.

Ten minutes past two.
Dos y diez.
dohs ee d'yess.

Ten minutes to three.
Tres menos diez.
trehs MEH-nohs d'yess.

At nine o'clock.
A las nueve.
ah lahs NWEH-veh.

At exactly nine o'clock.
A las nueve en punto.
ah lahs NWEH-veh er POON-toh.

the morning	**the afternoon**	**noon**
la mañana	la tarde	mediodía
la mahn-YA-na	*la TAR-deh*	*meh-d'yo-DEE-ya*

the night	**today**	**tomorrow**
la noche	hoy	mañana
la NO-cheh	*oy*	*mahn-YA-na*

yesterday	**the day after tomorrow**
ayer	pasado mañana
ah-YEHR	*pa-SA-doh mahn-YA-na*

the day before yesterday
anteayer
ahn-teh-ah-YEHR

this evening	**tomorrow evening**
esta noche	mañana por la noche
ESS-ta NO-cheh	*mahn-YA-na por la NO-cheh*

last night	**this week**
ayer por la noche	esta semana
ah-YEHR por la NO-cheh	*ESS-ta seh-MA-na*

last week	**next week**
la semana pasada	la semana próxima
la seh-MA-na pa-SA-da	*la seh-MA-na PROHX-see-ma.*

two weeks ago	**this month**
hace dos semanas	este mes
AH-seh dohs seh-MA-nas	*ESS-teh mess*

several months ago	**this year**
hace algunos meses	este año
AH-seh ahl-GOO-nohs MEH-sehs	*ESS-teh AHN-yo*

last year	**next year**
el año pasado	el año próximo
el AHN-yo pa-SA-doh	*el AHN-yo PROHX-see-mo*

five years ago	**1993**
hace cinco años	mil novecientos noventa y
AH-seh SEEN-ko AHN-yos	tres
	meel no-veh-S'YEN-tohs
	no-VEN-ta ee trehs

Monday	**Tuesday**	**Wednesday**
lunes	martes	miércoles
LOO-nehs	*MAR-tehs*	*M'YER-ko-lehs*

Thursday	**Friday**	**Saturday**	**Sunday**
jueves	viernes	sábado	domingo
HWEH-vehs	*V'YEHR-nehs*	*SA-ba-doh*	*doh-MEEN-go*

next Monday	**last Tuesday**	**on Fridays**
el lunes próximo	el martes pasado	los viernes
el LOO-nehs PROHX-see-mo	*el MAR-tehs pa-SA-doh*	*lohs V'YEHR-nehs*

January	**February**	**March**
enero	febrero	marzo
eh-NEH-ro	*feh-BREH-ro*	*MAR-so*

April	**May**	**June**
abril	mayo	junio
ah-BREEL	*MÁ-yo*	*HOON-yo*

July	**August**	**September**
julio	agosto	septiembre
HOOL-yo	*ah-GOHS-toh*	*set-T'YEM-breh*

October	**November**	**December**
octubre	noviembre	diciembre
ohk-TOO-breh	*no-V'YEM-breh*	*dee-S'YEM-breh*

On what date?	**March 1st**
¿En qué fecha?	El primero de marzo
¿en keh FEH-cha?	*el pree-MEH-ro deh MAR-so*

the 2nd	**the 3rd**	**the 4th** etc.
el dos	el tres	el cuatro
el dohs	*el trehs*	*el KWA-tro*

The 25th of December
El veinticinco de diciembre
el VAIN-tee-SEEN-ko deh dee-S'YEM-breh

Merry Christmas!
¡Feliz Navidad!
¡feh-LEESS nah-vee-DAHD!

The 1st of January
El primero de enero
el pree-MEH-ro deh eh-NEH-ro

Happy New Year!
¡Feliz Año Nuevo!
¡feh-LEESS AHN-yo NWEH-vo!

Congratulations!
¡Enhorabuena!
¡en-oh-ra-bweh-na!

Happy birthday!
¡Feliz cumpleaños!
¡feh-LEESS coom-pleh-AHN-yohs!

Independence Day
El día de la Independencia
el Dee-ah deh la een-deh-pen-DEN-s'ya

Long live ____!
¡Viva ____!
¡VEE-va ____!

A propósito: Spanish countries have different national holidays and many religious ones. The feast day of a particular saint is called **la fiesta de San** (or **Santa**) . . . followed by the saint's name. Such holidays vary according to country or city and are generally colorful and interesting to see.

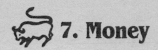 7. Money

Some Spanish-speaking countries use **pesos** with different values according to the country. Spain uses **pesetas,** and other countries give the **peso** a variety of names, sometimes taken from the names of national heroes—the **bolívar** in Venezuela, the **boliviano** in Bolivia, the **balboa** in Panama, the **sucre** in Ecuador—and somtimes from ancient Indian tradition, like the **sol** (sun) in Peru and the **quetzal** (a sacred bird) in Guatemala.

Where can I change money?
¿Dónde puedo cambiar dinero?
¿DOHN-deh PWEH-doh kahm-B'YAR dee-NEH-ro?

Can I change dollars here?
¿Puedo cambiar dólares aquí?
¿PWEH-doh kahm-B'YAR DOH-la-rehs ah-KEE?

Where is a bank?
¿Dónde hay un banco?
¿DOHN-deh I oon BAHN-ko?

What time does the bank open?
¿A qué hora abre el banco?
¿ah keh OH-ra AH-breh el BAHN-ko?

What time does the bank close?
¿A qué hora cierra el banco?
¿ah keh OH-ra S'YEH-rra el BAHN-ko?

What's the dollar rate?
¿A cómo está el cambio del dólar?
¿ah KO-mo ess-TA el KAHM-b'yo del DOH-lar?

Twelve pesos for one dollar.
Doce pesos por un dólar.
DOH-seh PEH-sohs por oon DOH-lar.

I want to change $50.
Quiero cambiar cincuenta dólares.
K'YEH-ro kahm-B'YAR seen-KWEN-ta DOH-la-rehs.

Do you accept traveler's checks?
¿Aceptan cheques de viajero?
¿ah-SEP-tahn CHEH-kehs deh v'ya-HEH-ro?

Of course.	**Not here.**
Desde luego.	Aquí no.
DEHS-deh L'WEH-go.	*ah-KEE no.*

Will you accept a personal check?
¿Aceptan un cheque personal?
¿ah-SEP-tahn oon CHEH-keh pehr-so-NAHL?

Have you identification?
¿Tiene Ud. identificación?
¿T'YEH-neh oo-STED ee-den-tee-fee-ka-S'YOHN?

Yes, here is my passport.
Sı, aquí está mi pasaporte.
see, ah-KEE ess-TA mee pa-sa-POR-teh.

Give me two 1000-peso notes.
Deme dos billetes de a mil pesos.
DEH-meh dohs beel-YEH-tehs deh ah meel PEH-sohs.

. . . ten 500-peso notes.	**. . . twenty 100 peso notes.**
. . . diez billetes de a quinientos.	. . . veinte billetes de a cien.
. . . *d'yess beel-YEH-tehs deh ah keen-YEN-tohs.*	. . . *veinte beel-YEH-tehs deh ah s'yen.*

I need change.
Necesito cambio.
neh-seh-SEE-toh KAHM-b'yo.

 **8. Basic Foods**

The foods and drinks mentioned in this section will enable you to be well fed in any Spanish-speaking country. The section that follows this will deal with special regional dishes of Spain and Latin America that you will encounter in your travels.

breakfast
desayuno
des-ah-YOO-no

orange juice
jugo de naranja
HOO-go deh na-RAHN-ha

grapefruit
toronja
toh-ROHN-ha

soft-boiled eggs
huevos passados por agua
WEH-vohs pa-SA-dohs por AH-gwa

fried eggs
huevos fritos
WEH-vohs FREE-tohs

an omelet
una tortilla de huevos
OO-na tor-TEEL-ya deh WEH-vohs

scrambled eggs
huevos revueltos
WEH-vohs rev-WEL-tohs

with bacon
con tocino
kohn toh-SEE-no

with ham
con jamón
kohn ha-MOHN

toast
tostadas
tohs-TA-dahs

coffee with (hot) milk
café con leche
ka-FEH kohn LEH-cheh

marmalade
mermelada
mehr-meh-LA-da

black coffee
café negro
ka-FEH NEH-gro

with cream
con crema
kohn KREH-ma

with sugar
con azúcar
kohn ah-SOO-kahr

cocoa
chocolate
cho-ko-LA-teh

tea
té
teh

with lemon
con limón
kohn lee-MOHN

lunch	**dinner**
almuerzo	cena
ahl-MWHER-so	*SEH-na*

Do you know a good restaurant?
¿Conoce Ud. un buen restaurante?
¿ko-NO-seh oo-STED oon bwehn rest-ow-RAHN-teh?

A table for three.	**This way, please**
Una mesa para tres.	Por aquí, por favor.
OO-na MEH-sa PA-ra trehs.	*por ah-KEE, por fa-VOR.*

The menu, please.	**What's good?**
El menú, por favor.	¿Qué hay de bueno?
el meh-NOO, por fa-VOR.	*¿keh I deh BWEH-no?*

What do you recommend?	**What is it?**
¿Qué recomienda Ud.?	¿Qué es?
¿keh re-ko-M'YEN-da oo-STED	*¿keh ess?*

Good.	**I'll try it.**	**Give me this.**
Bueno.	Lo probaré.	Deme esto.
BWEH-no.	*lo pro-ba-REH.*	*DEH-meh ESS-toh.*

First a cocktail.	**What is this?**
Primero un coctel.	¿Qué es esto?
pree-MEH-ro oon kohk-TEHL.	*¿keh ess ESS-toh?*

soup	**fish**	**oysters**
sopa	pescado	ostras
SO-pa	*pes-KA-doh*	*OHS-trahs*

shrimps	**lobster**
camarones	langosta
ka-ma-RO-nehs	*lahn-GOHS-ta*

roasted	**broiled**	**fried**	**boiled**
asado	a la parrilla	frito	hervido
ah-SA-doh	*ah la pa-REEL-ya*	*FREE-toh*	*ehr-VEE-doh*

roast chicken
pollo asado
*POHL-yo ah-
SA-doh*

fried chicken
pollo frito
*POHL-yo
FREE-toh*

turkey
pavo
PA-vo

duck
pato
PA-toh

roast pork
lechón asado
leh-CHOHN ah-SA-doh

pork chops
chuletas de cerdo
*choo-LEH-tahs deh SEHR-
doh*

veal chops
chuletas de ternera
choo-LEH-tahs deh ter-NEH-ra

lamp chops
chuletas de cordero
*choo-LEH-tahs deh kor-
DEH-ro*

roast lamb
cordero asado
kor-DEH-ro ah-SA-doh

beef
carne de res
*KAR-neh deh
ress*

steak
bistec
bees-TEK

hamburger
hamburguesa
ahm-boor-GEH-sa

well done
bien cocido
b'yen ko-SEE-doh

medium
término medio
TEHR-mee-no MEH-d'yo

rare
poco cocido
PO-ko ko-SEE-doh

very rare
casi crudo
KA-see KROO-doh

bread
pan
pahn

butter
mantequilla
*mahn-teh-KEEL-
ya*

rolls
panecillos
*pa-neh-SEEL-
yohs*

potatoes (Latin
America)
papas
PA-pahs

potatoes (Spain)
patatas
pa-TA-tahs

fried potatoes
papas fritas
*PA-pahs FREE-
tahs*

noodles	**rice**	**vegetables**	**green beans**
fideos	arroz	legumbres	habichuelas
fee-DEH-ohs	*ah-RROHS*	*leh-GOOM-bress*	*ah-bee-CHWEH-lahs*

peas (Spain)	**peas (Latin America)**	**carrots**
guisantes	petit pois	zanahorias
ghee-SAHN-tehs	*peh-tee PWA*	*sa-na-OHR-yahs*

spinach	**cabbage**	**onions**	**mushrooms**
espinaca	repollo	cebollas	setas
ess-pee-NA-ka	*reh-POHL-yo*	*seh-BOHL-yahs*	*SEH-tahs*

asparagus	**salad**	**oil**	**vinegar**
espárrago	ensalada	aceite	vinagre
ess-PA-rra-go	*en-sa-LA-da*	*ah-SAY-teh*	*vee-NA-greh*

salt	**pepper**	**mustard**	**spicy sauce**
sal	pimienta	mostaza	salsa picante
sahl	*pee-M'YEN-ta*	*mo-STA-sah*	*SAHL-sa pee-KAHN-teh*

Which wine do you recommend?
¿Qué vino recomienda?
¿keh VEE-no reh-ko-M'YEN-da?

white wine	**red wine**
vino blanco	vino tinto
VEE-no BLAHN-ko	*VEE-no TEEN-toh*

beer	**champagne**	**To your health!**
cerveza	champaña	¡A su salud!
sehr-VEH-sa	*chahm-PAHN-ya*	*¡ah soo sa-LOOD!*

fruits **grapes** **peaches** **apples**
frutas uvas melocotones manzanas
FROO-tahs *OO-vahs* *me-lo-ko-* *mahn-SA-*
TOH-nehs *nahs*

pears **bananas** **pineapples**
peras plátanos piñas
PEH-rahs *PLA-ta-nohs* *PEEN-yahs*

strawberries **oranges**
fresas naranjas
FREH-sahs *na-RAHN-hahs*

a dessert **pastry** **cake**
un postre pastelería torta
oon POHS-treh *pas-teh-leh-REE-ya* *TOR-ta*

ice cream **cheese**
helado queso
eh-LA-doh *KEH-so*

coffee **demitasse**
café café solo
ka-FEH *ka-FEH SO-lo*

More, please.
Más, por favor.
mahs, por fa-VOR.

That's enough, thank you.
Suficiente, gracias.
soo-fee-S'YEN-teh, GRA-s'yahs.

Waiter! **Waitress!**
¡Camarero! ¡Camarera!
¡ka-ma-REH-ro! *¡ka-ma-REH-ra!*

The check, please.
La cuenta, por favor.
la KWEN-ta, por fa-VOR.

Is the tip included?
¿Está incluída la propina?
¿ess-TA een-kloo-EE-da la pro-PEE-na?

I think the bill is incorrect.
Creo que la cuenta está incorrecta.
KREH-oh keh la KWEN-ta ess-TA een-ko-RREK-ta.

Oh no, sir.	**Look here.**	**You see?**
Oh no, señor.	Mire aquí.	¿Ve Ud.?
oh no, sen-YOR.	*MEE-reh ah-KEE*	*¿veh oo-STED?*

Yes, it's true.   **It's O.K.**
Sí, es verdad.   Está bien.
see, ess ver-DAHD.   *ess-TA b'yen.*

Come again soon.
Vuelva pronto.
VWEL-va PROHN-toh.

POINT TO THE ANSWER

To make sure you understand the menu, show the following section to the waiter so that he can select the answer. The sentence in Spanish after the arrow asks him to point out the answer.

 Tenga la bondad de indicar aquí abajo su contestación a mi pregunta. Muchísimas gracias.

Esta es nuestra specialidad.
This is our specialty.

Está listo.	**No está listo.**
It's ready.	It isn't ready.

Se necesita un cuarto de hora.
It takes a quarter of an hour.

Esto se sirve sólo los viernes.
That is served only on Fridays.

Es pollo,	It's chicken,
cerdo,	pork,
puerco,	pork,
cordero,	lamb,
ternera,	veal,
res,	beef,
cabrito,	young goat,
pescado,	fish,
mariscos,	seafood,

. . . con legumbres.	**en una salsa.**
. . . with vegetables.	. . . in a sauce.

9. Food Specialties of the Spanish World

These expressions and names of dishes will be useful in restaurants or private homes where you may be invited. These dishes commonly appear on most Spanish or Latin American menus and are so much a part of Spanish and Latin American dining tradition that you should recognize them and know how to pronounce them as well as to enjoy them. We have written the Spanish names first, since that is how you will see them on the menu.

What is today's special?
¿Cuál es el plato del día?
¿kwahl ess el PLA-toh del DEE-ya

Is it ready?
¿Está listo?
¿ess-TA LEES-toh?

How long will it take?
¿Cuánto tiempo demora?
¿KWAHN-toh T'YEM-po deh-MO-ra?

Gazpacho andaluz
gahs-PA-cho ahn-da-LOOSS
Cold soup of raw onions, cucumber, tomatoes, garlic, oil, and vinegar.

Caldo gallego
KAHL-doh ghal-YEH-go
Soup of meat and vegetables

Puchero
poo-CHEH-roo
Thick soup of meat, corn, and other vegetables

Calamares en su tinta
ka-la-MA-rehs en soo TEEN-ta
Squids cooked in their black juice

Bacalao a la vizcaína
ba-kahl-OW ah la vees-ka-EE-na
Salt codfish with onions, peppers, and tomato sauce

Filetes de lenguado empanados
fee-LEH-tehs deh len-GWA-doh em-pa-NA-dohs
Breaded fillet of sole

Zarzuela
sar-SWEH-la
Assorted shellfish, stewed

Fabada
fa-BA-da
Stew of sausage, pork, bacon, and beans

Arroz con pollo
ah-RROHS kohn POHL-yo
Chicken steamed with rice, onions, tomatoes, and saffron

Paella valenciana
pa-EL-ya va-len-S'YA-na
Chicken, sausage, mussels, clams, lobster, peppers,
   onions, tomatoes, and saffron rice

Pollo en cazuela
POHL-yo en ka-SWEH-la
Stew of chicken and vegetables

Lechón asado
leh-CHOHN ah-SA-doh
Roast suckling pig

Ropa vieja
RO-pa V'YEH-ha
Braised beef with tomato and pimiento sauce

Picadillo
pee-ka-DEEL-yo
Chopped beef and pork steamed with tomatoes, onions,
   and peppers

Mole de guajalote
MO-leh deh gwa-ha-LO-teh
Turkey with sauce of bitter chocolate and hot peppers

Enchiladas
en-chee-LA-dahs
Cornmeal pancakes filled with meat and chili sauce, raw
onions, and grated cheese

Moros y cristianos ("Moors and Christians")
MO-rohs ee krees-T'YA-nohs
Black beans, rice, diced ham, peppers, tomatoes, and
garlic

Huevos rancheros
WEH-vohs ran-CHEH-rohs
Fried eggs with chili sauce, raw onion, grated cheese, and
tortillas

Jamón serrano
ha-MOHN seh-RRA-no
Thin-sliced smoked ham

Guacamole
gwa-ka-MO-leh
Avocado mashed with hot peppers, onions, tomatoes, lime
juice, and garlic

Flan
flahn
Caramel custard

Cascos de guayaba con queso
KAHS-kohs deh gwa-YA-ba kohn KEH-so
Preserved guava with cream cheese

How do you like it?	It's delicious!
¿Cómo le parece?	¡Está delicioso!
¿KO-mo leh pa-REH-seh?	¡ess-TA deh-lee-S'YO-so!

It's very tasty!
¡Está riquísimo!
¡ess-TA ree-KEE-see-mo!

What is it called?
¿Cómo se llama?
¿KO-mo seh L'YA-ma?

This is my favorite dish.
Este es mi plato favorito.
Ess-teh ess mee PLA-toh fa-vo-REE-toh

The dessert is excellent.
El postre es excelente.
el POHS-treh ess ek-seh-LEN-teh.

Thank you for a wonderful dinner!
¡Mil gracias por una cena exquisita!
¡meel GRA-s'yahs por OO-na SEH-na es-kee-SEE-ta!

You are welcome.
Por nada.
por NA-da.

I'm happy that you enjoyed it.
Encantado que le haya gustado.
en-kahn-TA-doh keh leh AH-ya goo-STA-doh.

10. Transportation

Getting around by public transportation is enjoyable not only for the new and interesting things you see, but also because of the opportunities you have for practicing Spanish. To make your travels easier, use short phrases when speaking to drivers or others when you ask directions. And don't forget **Por favor** and **Gracias!**

Bus

Where is the bus stop?
¿Dónde está la parada de autobús?
¿DOHN-deh ess-TA la pa-Ra-da deh ow-toh-BOOSS?

Do you go to the Plaza Mayor?
¿Ud. va a la Plaza Mayor?
¿oo-STED va ah la PLA-sa ma-YOR?

No, take number nine.
No, tome el número nueve.
no, TOH-meh el NOO-meh-ro NWEH-veh.

How much is the fare?
¿Cuánto es el pasaje?
¿KWAHN-toh ess el pa-SA-heh?

Where do you want to go?
¿Adónde quiere ir?
¿ah-DOHN-deh K'YEH-reh eer?

To the cathedral.
A la catedral.
ah la ka-teh-DRAHL.

Is it far?
¿Está lejos?
¿ess-TA LEH-hohs

No, it's near.
No, está cerca.
no, ess-TA SEHR-ka.

Please tell me where to get off.
Dígame, por favor, dónde debo bajar.
DEE-ga-meh, por fa-VOR, DOHN-deh DEH-bo ba-HAR.

Do I get off here?
¿Bajo aquí?
¿BA-ho ah-KEE?

POINT TO THE ANSWER

To make sure you understand the answer to the question you have asked, show the following section to the bus driver or conductor so that the person can select the answer. The sentence in Spanish after the arrow asks the bus driver or conductor to point out the answer.

> *Tenga la bondad de indicar aquí abajo su contestación a mi pregunta. Muchísimas gracias.*

Baje aquí.   **Allá.**   **Por allá.**
Get off here.   Over there.   That way.

En la esquina.   **En el otro lado de la calle.**
At the corner.   On the other side of the
                     street.

A la derecha.   **A la izquierda.**
To the right.   To the left.

Derecho.   **No sé.**
Straight ahead.   I don't know.

Taxi

Taxi.
Taxi.
TAHX-see.

Are you free?
¿Está libre?
¿ess-TA LEE-breh?

Where to?
¿Adónde vamos?
¿ah-DOHN-deh VA-mohs?

To this address.
A esta dirección.
ah ESS-ta dee-rek-
·S'YOHN.

Do you know where it is?
¿Sabe dónde está?
¿SA-beh DOHN-deh ess-
TA?

I am in a hurry.
Tengo prisa.
TEN-go PREE-sa.

Go faster!
¡Vaya más rápido!
¡VA-ya mahs RAHP-ee-
doh!

Slower!
¡Más despacio!
¡mahs dess-PA-s'yo!

Stop here.
Para aquí.
PA-reh ah-KEE.

At the corner.
En la esquina.
En la ess-KEE-na.

How much is it?
¿Cuánto es?
¿KWAHN-toh ess?

Wait for me.
Espéreme.
ess-PEH-reh-meh.

I'll be back soon.
Volveré pronto.
vohl-veh-REH PROHN-
toh.

In five minutes.
En cinco minutos.
en SEEN-ko mee-NOO-
tohs.

O.K., I'll wait for you.
Está bien, le espero.
ess-TA b'yen, leh ess-PEH-ro.

How much is it by the hour?
¿Cuánto es por hora?
¿KWAHN-toh ess por OH-ra?

. . . per kilometer?
. . . por kilómetro?
. . . por kee-LO-meh-tro?

Call for me tomorrow.
Venga mañana a buscarme.
VEN-ga mahn-YA-na ah boo-SKAR-meh.

In the morning.	**In the afternoon.**
Por la mañana.	Por la tarde.
por la mahn-YA-na.	*por la TAR-deh.*

At 3 o'clock.	**At the hotel _____.**
A las tres.	En el hotel _____.
ah lahs trehs.	*en el o-TEL _____.*

A propósito: Tip 10% of the meter, but for longer trips make arrangements *before* you start. Some cities have taxis that operate along a specified street like small buses and charge a nominal sum to each of the various passengers they pick up. This is a good way to cut down on taxi fares as well as to improve your Spanish.

POINT TO THE ANSWER

To make sure you understand the answer to a question you have asked a taxi driver, show the driver the following section. The sentence in Spanish after the arrow asks the driver to point out the answer.

> *Tenga la bondad de indicar aquí abajo su contestación a mi pregunta. Muchísimas gracias.*

Le esperaré aquí.
I'll wait for you here.

No puedo esperar.
I can't wait.

Aquí no se puede estacionar.
You can't park here.

Volveré para buscarlo.
I'll be back to pick you up.

No es suficiente.   **El equipaje es extra.**
It's not enough.   The baggage is extra.

Train and Subway

Is there a subway in this city?
¿Hay subterráneo en esta ciudad?
¿I soob-teh-RRA-neh-yo en ESS-ta s'yoo-DAHD?

Where is the subway?
¿Dónde está el subterráneo?
¿DOHN-deh ess-TA el soob-teh-RRA-neh-yo?

Where is the railroad station?
¿Dónde está la estación de ferrocarriles?
*¿DOHN-deh ess-TA la ess-ta-S'YOHN
deh feh-rro-ka-RREEL-lehs?*

Where do I buy the tickets?
¿Dónde se compran los billetes?
¿DOHN-deh seh KOHM-prahn lohs beel-YEH-tess?

One ticket for Granada.
Un billete para Granada.
oon beel-YEH-teh PA-ra gra-NA-da.

Round trip.   **One way only.**
Ida y vuelta.   Ida solamente.
EE-da ee VWEL-ta.   *EE-da so-la-MEN-teh.*

First class.
Primera clase.
pree-MEH-ra KLA-seh.

Second class.
Segunda clase.
seh-GOON-da KLA-seh.

A timetable.
Un itinerario.
oon ee-tee-neh-RA-r'yo.

Where is the train for Santiago?
¿Dónde está el tren para Santiago?
¿DOHN-deh ess-TA el trehn PA-ra sahn-T'YA-go?

On what platform is the train?
¿En que andén está el tren?
¿en keh ahn-DEHN ess-TA el trehn?

When do we leave?
¿Cuándo salimos?
¿KWAHN-doh sa-LEE-mohs?

Is this seat taken?
¿Está ocupado este asiento?
¿ess-TA oh-koo-PA-doh ESS-teh ah-S'YEN-toh?

With your permission, madam.
Con permiso, señora.
kohn per-MEE-so, sen-YO-ra.

Of course, sir.
¡Cómo no, señor!
¡KO-mo no, sen-YOR!

At what time do we get to Veracruz?
¿A qué hora llegamos a Veracruz?
¿ah keh OH-ra l'yeh-GA-mohs ah veh-ra-KROOSS?

Does the train stop in Puebla?
¿Se para el tren en Puebla?
¿seh PA-ra el trehn en PWEH-bla?

How long are we stopping here?
¿Cuánto tiempo demoramos aquí?
¿KWAHN-toh T'YEM-po deh-mo-RA-mohs ah-KEE?

Where is the dining car?
¿Dónde está el coche comedor?
¿DOHN-deh ess-TA el-KO-cheh ko-meh-DOR?

I can't find my ticket.
No puedo encontrar mi billete.
no PWEH-doh en-kohn-TRAR mee beel-YEH-teh.

Wait!   **Here it is!**
¡Espere!   ¡Aquí está!
¡ess-PEH-reh!   *¡ah-KEE ess-TA!*

Prepare my berth, please.
Prepare mi camarote, por favor.
preh-PA-reh mee ka-mu-RO-teh, por fa-VOR.

Can you help me?   **I want to go to _____.**
¿Puede ayudarme?   Quiero ir a _____.
¿PWEH-deh ah-yoo-DAR-   *K'YEH-ro eer ah _____.*
meh?

I took the wrong train.
Tomé el tren equivocado.
toh-MEH el trehn eh-kee-vo-KA-doh.

POINT TO THE ANSWER

To make sure you understand the answer to a question
you have asked about trains show the following section to
a conductor or station guard so that the person can select
the answer. The sentence in Spanish after the arrow asks
the conductor or station guard to point out the answer.

> *Tenga la bondad de indicar aquí abajo su*
> *contestación a mi pregunta. Muchísimas*
> *gracias.*

La vía numero ____. Track number ____.	Por allí. That way.	Abajo. Downstairs	Arriba. Upstairs.

Este no es el tren suyo.
This is not your train.

Here it is!
¡Aquí está!

Sale en ____ minutos.
It leaves in ____ minutes.

Llegamos a las ____.
We arrive at ____ o'clock.

Ship

To the dock.
Al muelle.
ahl MWEL-l'yeh.

Can one go on board now?
¿Se puede ir a bordo ahora?
¿seh PWEH-deh eer ah BOR-doh ah-OH-ra?

At what time does the ship sail?
¿A qué hora zarpa el barco?
¿ah keh OH-ra SAR-pa el BAR-ko?

From which pier?
¿De qué muelle?
¿deh keh MWEL-l'yeh?

Pardon me. Where is cabin B-29?
Perdón. ¿Dónde está el camarote B-29?
pehr-DOHN. ¿DOHN-deh ess-TA el kama-RO-teh beh VAIN-tee-N'WEH-veh?

The sea is rough, isn't it?
El mar está picado, ¿verdad?
el mar ess-TA pee-KA-doh, ¿vehr-DAHD?

I feel seasick.
Me siento mareado. (m) . . . mareada. (f)
meh S'YEN-toh ma-reh-AH-doh. . . . ma-reh-AH-da.

Does the boat stop in La Guaira?
¿Para el barco en La Guaira?
¿PA-ra el BAR-ko en la G'WY-ra?

11. Traveling by Automobile

Car Rental

Where can one rent a car?
¿Dónde se puede alquilar un auto?
¿DOHN-deh seh PWEH-deh ahl-kee-LAR oon OW-toh?

. . . a motorcycle?
. . . una motocicleta?
. . . OO-na mo-toh-see-KLEH-ta?

. . . a bicycle?
. . . una bicicleta?
. . . OO-na bee-see-KLEH-ta?

I want to rent a car.
Quiero alquilar un auto.
K'YEH-ro ahl-kee-LAR oon OW-toh.

How much per day?
¿Cuánto cuesta por día?
¿KWAHN-toh KWESS-ta por DEE-ya?

How much per kilometer?
¿Cuánto cuesta por kilómetro?
¿KWAHN-toh KWESS-ta por kee-LO-meh-tro?

Is the gasoline included?
¿Está incluída la gasolina?
¿ess-TA een-kloo-EE-da la gas-so-LEE-na?

Is the transmission automatic?
¿Es de cambio automático?
¿ess deh KAHM-b'yo ow-toh-MA-tee-ko?

I would like to try it out.
Me gustaría probarlo.
meh goo-sta-REE-ya pro-BAR-lo.

A propósito: The word for "car" is **coche** in Spain, and **carro** in Latin America. In Spain **carro** means "cart," while in Latin America **coche** means "coach." "Automobile" is **automóvil** or **auto** in all Spanish-speaking countries.

Distances are reckoned in kilometers, approximately ⅝ of a mile.

Gas Station

Where can one buy gasoline?
¿Dónde se puede comprar gasolina?
¿DOHN-deh seh PWEH-deh kohm-PRAR gas-so-LEE-na?

How much per liter?*
¿Cuánto es por litro?
‹KWAHN-toh ess por LEE-tro?
* Gas is sold by the liter (1.05 quarts). In other words, four liters is about one gallon.

Thirty liters, please.	**Fill it up.**
Treinta litros, por favor.	Llénelo.
TRAIN-ta LEE-trohs, por fa-VOR.	*L'YEH-neh-lo.*

Please . . . put air in the tires.
Por favor . . . ponga aire en las llantas.
por fa-VOR . . . PON-ga I-reh en lahs L'YAHN-tahs

Look at the water.	**. . . the battery.**
Vea el agua.	. . . la batería.
VEH-ah el AH-gwa.	*. . . la ba-teh-REE-ya.*

. . . the oil.	**. . . the spark plugs.**
. . . el aceite	. . . las bujías.
. . . el ah-SAY-teh.	*. . . lahs boo-HEE-yahs.*

. . . the brakes.
. . . los frenos.
. . . lohs FREH-nohs.

. . . the carburetor.
. . . el carburador.
. . . el kar-boo-ra-DOR.

Change the oil.
Cambie el aceite.
KAHM-b'yeh el ah-SAY-teh.

Grease the motor.
Engrase el motor.
en-GRA-seh el mo-TOR.

Change this tire.
Cambie esta llanta.
*KAHM-b'yeh ESS-ta
L'YAHN-ta.*

Wash the car.
Lave el auto.
LA-veh el OW-toh.

A road map, please.
Un mapa de carreteras, por
favor.
*oon MA-pa deh ka-rreh-
TEH-rahs, por fa-VOR.*

Where is the restroom?
¿Dónde está el excusado?
¿DOHN-deh ess-TA el ess-koo-SA-doh?

Asking Directions

Where does this road go to?
¿Adónde va esta carretera?
¿ah-DOHN-deh va ESS-ta ka-rreh-TEH-ra?

Is this the way to Mérida?
¿Es éste el camino para Mérida?
¿ess ESS-teh el ka-MEE-no PA-ra MEH-ree-da?

Is the road good?
¿Está bueno el camino?
¿ess-TA BWEH-no el ka-MEE-no?

Which is the road to San José?
¿Cuál el la vía para San José?
¿kwahl ess la VEE-ya PA-ra sahn ho-SEH?

It's that way.
Es por allí.
ess por ahl-YEE.

Is the next town far?
¿Está lejos el próximo pueblo?
¿ess-TA LEH-hohs el PROHX-see-mo PWEH-blo?

Do you know if there is a good restaurant there?
¿Sabe Ud. si hay un buen restaurante allí?
*¿SA-beh oo-STED see I oon bwehn rest-ow-RAHN-teh ahl-
   YEE?*

Is there a good hotel in Arequipa?
¿Hay un buen hotel en Arequipa?
¿I oon bwehn o-TEL en ah-reh-KEE-pa?

POINT TO THE ANSWER

To make sure you understand the answer to a question you
have asked about roads and directions show the following
section to a Spanish-speaking person so that he or she can
select the answer. The sentence in Spanish after the arrow
asks him or her to point to the answer.

> *Tenga la bondad de indicar aquí abajo su
> contestación a mi pregunta. Muchísimas
> gracias.*

Nosotros estamos en este punto en este mapa.
We are at this point on this map.

El próximo pueblo se llama _____.
The next town is called _____.

No está lejos.
It's not far.

_____ kilómetros, más o menos.
_____ kilometers, more or less.

Siga este camino.
Follow this road.

En el próximo semáforo,
At the next traffic signal,

—doble a la derecha.
—turn right.

Después de atravesar el puente
After you cross the bridge

—doble a la izquierda.
—turn left.

Entonces siga derecho.
Then go straight ahead.

Siga hasta llegar a la autopista.
Continue until you come to the expressway.

Pero, tenga cuidado.
But be careful.

Hay limite de velocidad.
There's a speed limit.

Emergencies and Repairs

Your license!
¡Su licencia!
¡soo lee-SEN-s'ya!

Here it is, officer.
Aquí está, señor agente.
ah-KEE ess-TA, sen-YOR ah-HEN-teh.

And the registration.
Y la matrícula.
ee la ma-TREE-koo-la.

It wasn't my fault.
No fue culpa mía.
no fweh KOOL-pa MEE-ah.

The truck skidded.
El camión patinó.
el ka-mee-OHN pa-tee-NO.

This imbecile crashed into me.
Este imbécil me chocó.
ESS-teh eem-BEH-seel meh cho-KO.

A propósito: As the Spanish drive with considerable dash and challenge, **imbécil, idiota,** and **bruto** are frequent and even rather mild expletives. However, control and good humor, plus a diplomatic use of Spanish, will make car travel safe and very enjoyable.

I am in trouble.
Estoy en un apuro.
ess-TOY en oon ah-POO-ro.

My car has broken down.
Mi coche se ha descompuesto.
mee KO-cheh seh ah des-kohm-PWESS-toh.

Could you help me?
¿Podría ayudarme?
¿po-DREE-ya ah-yoo-DAR-meh?

I have a flat tire.
Tengo una llanta pinchada.
TEN-goo OO-na L'YAHN-ta peen-CHA-da.

Can you lend me a jack?
¿Puede prestarme un gato?
¿PWEH-deh press-TAR-meh oon GA-toh?

It's stuck.
Está atascado.
ess-TA ah-tahs-KA-doh.

Can you push me?
¿Puede empujarme?
¿PWEH-deh em-poo-HAR-meh?

A thousand thanks!
¡Mil gracias!
¡meel GRA-s'yahs!

You are very kind.
Ud. es muy amable.
oo-STED ess mwee ah-MA-bleh.

I want to see the mechanic.
Quiero ver al mecánico.
K'YEH-ro vehr ahl meh-KA-nee-ko.

He doesn't work on weekends.
No trabaja los fines de semana.
no tra-BA-ha los FEE-nehs deh seh-MA-na.

What's the matter?
¿Qué pasa?
¿keh PA-sa?

The car doesn't go well.
El carro no anda bien.
el KA-rro no AHN-da b'yen.

There is a funny noise in the motor.
Hay un ruido raro en el motor.
I oon RWEE-doh RA-ro en el mo-TOR.

It's difficult to start.
Arranca con dificultad.
ah-RAHN-ka kohn dee-fee-kool-TAHD

Can you fix it?
¿Puede arreglarlo?
¿PWEH-deh ah-rreh-GLAR-lo?

What will it cost?
¿Cuánto costará?
¿KWAHN-toh kohs-ta-RA?

How long will it take?
¿Cuánto tiempo tomará?
¿KWAHN-toh T'YEM-po toh-ma-RA?

When will it be ready?
¿Cuándo estará listo?
¿KWAHN-doh ess-ta-RA LEES-toh?

I'm in a hurry.
Tengo prisa.
TEN-go PREE-sa.

A propósito: For making sure exactly when the car will be ready, consult the phrases in the "Time" section, page 23.

POINT TO THE ANSWER

To make sure you understand the answer to a question you have asked about car repairs show the following section to the mechanic to select the answer. The sentence in Spanish after the arrow asks the mechanic to point to the answer.

 Tenga la bondad de indicar aquí abajo su contestación a mi pregunta. Muchísimas gracias.

Esto le saldrá a ＿＿ pesos.
It will cost you ＿＿ pesos.

Estará listo en ＿＿ horas.
It will be ready in ＿＿ hours.

Hoy no es posible.   **Quizá mañana.**
Today it isn't possible.   Perhaps tomorrow.

No tenemos la pieza.
We don't have the part.

Podemos repararlo temporariamente.
We can repair it temporarily.

También necesita una llanta nueva.
You also need a new tire.

(Certain Spanish words vary from country to country. *Tire,* for example, is called *llanta, goma,* or *neumático* in various parts of the Spanish world, and gas for a car is called, according to area, *gasolina, benzina, petróleo,* or *carburante. Car* is *coche* in Spain and *carro* in Spanish America.) In addition you will hear or see the following instructions:

GUARDE SU DERECHA
GWAHR-deh soo deh-
REH-cha
Keep to the right

DESVÍO
des-VEE-yo
Detour

UNA VÍA
OO-na VEE-ya
One way

ENCRUCIJADA
Enn-kroo-see-HA-da
Crossroads

VELOCIDAD MÁXIMA ＿＿＿KM.
veh-lo-see-DAHD MAHX-ee-ma ＿＿＿ kee-LO-meh-trohs
Maximum speed ＿＿＿ kilometers

SE PROHIBE
ESTACIONAR
seh-pro-EE-beh ess-ta-s'yo-
NAR
No parking

CURVA
KOOR-va
Curve

OBRAS EN PROGRESO
OH-brahs en pro-GREH-so
Work in progress

REDUZCA LA
VELOCIDAD
re-DOOS-ka la veh-lo-see-
DAHD
Reduce speed

ENTRADA
en-TRA-da
Entrance

SALIDA
sa-LEE-da
Exit

PEATONES
peh-ah-TOH-nehs
Pedestrians

PROHIBIDO EL PASO A BICICLETAS
pro-ee-BEE-doh el PA-so ah bee-see-KLEH-tahs
No bicycles

PELIGRO
peh-LEE-gro
Danger

TENGA CUIDADO
TEN-ga kwee-DA-doh
Be careful

International Road Signs

DANGER

CAUTION

SHARP TURN

CROSSROADS

RIGHT CURVE

LEFT CURVE

**GUARDED
RR CROSSING**

**UNGUARDED
RR CROSSING**

**MAIN ROAD
AHEAD**

BUMPS

ONE WAY

DO NOT ENTER

NO PARKING

PARKING

CRUCE DE FERROCARRIL
KROO-seh deh feh-rro-ka-RREEL
Railroad crossing

CARRETERA PRINCIPAL ADELANTE
ka-rreh-TEH-ra preen-see-PAHL ah-deh-LAHN-teh
Main road ahead

CURVA A LA DERECHA
KOOR-va ah la deh-REH-cha
Right curve

CURVA A LA IZQUIERDA
KOOR-va ah la eez-K'YEHR-da
Left curve

12. Sightseeing and Photography

We have combined these two important sections since you will want to take pictures of what you are seeing. If you are taking pictures indoors, be sure to ask the custodian **¿Está permitido?**—"Is it permitted?"

Sightseeing

I need a guide.
Necesito un guía.
neh-seh-SEE-toh oon GHEE-ya.

Are you a guide?
¿Es Ud. guía?
¿ess oo-STED GHEE-ya?

Do you speak English?
¿Habla Ud. inglés?
¿AH-bla oo-STED een-GLEHS?

It doesn't matter.
No importa.
no eem-POR-ta.

I speak a little Spanish.
Hablo un poco de español.
AH-blo oon PO-ko de ess-pahn-YOHL.

Do you have a car?
¿Tiene auto?
¿T'YEH-neh OW-toh?

How much do you charge per hour?
¿Cuánto cobra por hora?
¿KWAHN-toh KO-bra por OH-ra?

How much per day?
¿Cuánto por día?
¿KWAHN-toh por DEE-ya?

For two people?
¿Para dos personas?
¿PA-rah dohs pehr-SO-nahs?

A group of four?
¿Un grupo de cuatro?
¿oon GROO-po deh KWA-tro?

We would like to see the old part of the city.
Nos gustaría ver la parte antigua de la ciudad.
*nohs goo-sta-REE-ya vehr la PAR-teh ahn-TEE-gwa deh
la s'yoo-DAHD.*

Where is the Bull Ring?
¿Dónde queda la Plaza de Toros?
¿DOHN-deh KEH-da la PLA-sa deh TOH-rohs?

We want to go . . .   **. . . to the Prado Museum.**
Queremos ir . . .   . . . al Museo del Prado.
keh-REH-mohs eer . . .   *. . . ahl moo-SEH-oh del
                                PRA-doh.*

. . . to the Plaza San Martín.
. . . a la plaza San Martín.
. . . a la PLA-sa sahn mar-TEEN.

. . . to the central park.
. . . al parque central.
. . . ahl PAHR-keh sen-TRAHL.

. . . to the zoo.
. . . al jardín zoológico.
. . . ahl har-DEEN so-oh-LO-hee-ko.

. . . to the San Juan market.
. . . al mercado de San Juan.
. . . ahl mehr-KA-doh deh sahn hwahn.

. . . to see the archaeological excavations.
. . . a ver las excavaciones arqueológicas.
. . . a vehr lahs ex-ka-vah-S'YO-nehs ar-keh-oh-LO-hee-kahs.

. . . to the royal palace.
. . . al palacio real.
. . . ahl pa-LA-s'yo reh-AHL.

How beautiful!   **Very interesting!**
¡Qué bello!   ¡Muy interesante!
¡keh BEL-yo!   *¡mwee een-teh-reh-SAHN-
                            teh!*

From what period is this?
¿De qué época es esto?
¿deh keh EH-po-ka ess ESS-toh?

Do you know a good   **Let's go.**
  nightclub?   Vamos.
¿Conoce un buen club   *VA-mohs.*
  nocturno?
¿ko-NO-seh oon bwehn
  kloob nohk-TOOR-no?

You are a very good guide.
Ud. es un guía muy bueno.
oo-STED ess oon GHEE-ya mwee BWEH-no.

Come again tomorrow.   **At 9 o'clock.**
Vuelva mañana.   A las nueve.
VWEL-va mahn-YA-na.   *ah lahs NWEH-veh.*

And, if you don't have a guide:

May one enter?   **It is open.**
¿Se puede entrar?   Está abierto.
¿seh PWEH-deh en-TRAR?   *ess-TA ah-B'YEHR-toh.*

It is closed.
Está cerrado.
ess-TA seh-RRA-doh.

What are the visiting hours?
¿Cuáles son las horas de visita?
¿KWAH-lehs sohn lahs OH-rahs deh vee-SEE-ta?

It opens at 2 o'clock.
Abre a las dos.
AH-breh ah lahs dohs.

It is closed for repairs.
Está cerrado por reparaciones.
ess-TA seh-RRA-doh por reh-pa-ra-S'YO-nehs.

Can one take photos?
¿Se puede tomar fotografías?
¿seh PWEH-deh toh-MAR- fo-toh-gra-FEE-yahs?

It is permitted.
Está permitido.
ess-TA pehr-mee-TEE-doh.

It is forbidden.
Está prohibido.
ess-TA pro-ee-BEE-doh.

Leave your packages in the checkroom.
Deje sus paquetes en el guardarropa.
DEH-heh soos pa-KEH-tehs en el gwahr-da-RRO-pa.

What is the admission?
¿Cuánto cuesta la entrada?
KWAHN-toh KWES-ta la en-TRA-da?

Two pesos 50 centavos.
Dos pesetas cincuenta.
dohs peh-SEH-tahs seen-KWEN-ta.

And, for children?
Y, ¿para niños?
ee, ¿PA-ra NEEN-yohs?

The admission is free.
La entrada es gratis.
la en-TRA-da ess GRA-teess.

Your ticket, please.
Su billete, por favor.
soo beel-YEH-teh, por fa-VOR.

Follow me.
Sígame.
SEE-ga-meh.

No smoking.
Prohibido fumar.
Pro-ee-BEE-doh foo-MAR.

This way, please.
Por aquí, por favor.
por ah-KEE, por fa-VOR.

This castle . . .
Este castillo . . .
ESS-teh kahs-TEEL-yo . . .

This palace . . .
Este palacio . . .
ESS-teh pa-LA-s'yo . . .

This church . . .
Esta iglesia . . .
ESS-ta ee-GLEH-s'ya. . .

This monument . . .
Este monumento . . .
ESS-teh mo-noo-MEN-toh . . .

This street . . .
Esta calle . . .
ESS-ta KAHL-yeh . . .

This square . . .
Esta plaza . . .
ESS-ta PLA-sa . . .

What is it called?
¿Cómo se llama?
¿KO-mo seh l'ya-ma?

It's magnificent!
¡Es magnífico!
¡ess mahg-NEE-fee-ko!

It's very interesting!
¡Es muy interesante!
¡es mwee een-teh-reh-SAHN-teh!

It's very old, isn't it?
Es muy antiguo, ¿verdad?
ess mwee ahn-TEE-gwo, ¿vehr-DAHD?

This is for you.
Esto es para Ud.
ESS-toh ess PA-ra oo-STED.

Some signs you may see in public places:

CABALLEROS or
ka-bahl-
  YEH-rohs
Gentlemen

HOMBRES
OHM-brehs
Men

DAMAS
DA-mahs
Ladies

ENTRADA
en-TRA-da
Entrance

SALIDA
sa-LEE-da
Exit

ABIERTO
*ah-B'YEHR-
  toh*
Open

CERRADO
seh-RRA-doh
Closed

**HORAS DE
  VISITA**
*OH-rahs deh vee-
  SEE-ta*
Visiting hours

INFORMACIÓN
*een-for-ma-
  S'YOHN*
Information

VESTUARIO
ves-TWA-r'yo
Checkroom

CALIENTE
ka-L'YEN-teh
Hot

FRÍO
FREE-yo
Cold

TIRE
TEE-reh
Pull

EMPUJE
em-POO-heh
Push

SE PROHIBE ENTRAR
seh pro-EE-beh en-TRAR
No admittance

SE PROHIBE FUMAR
seh pro-EE-beh foo-MAR
No smoking

ESTÁ PROHIBIDO FIJAR CARTELES
ess-TA pro-ee-BEE-doh fee-HAR kar-TEH-lehs
No sign posting

A propósito: The term **prohibido** or **se prohibe** in signs has the general connotation of "No" or "Don't do it"; so when you see these words, don't walk on the grass, smoke, take photographs, or whatever the case may be.

Photography

Where is the camera shop?
¿Dónde hay una tienda de efectos de fotografía?
¿DOHN-deh I OO-na T'YEN-da deh eh-FEK-tohs deh fo-toh-gra-FEE-ya?

I would like a roll (of film)
Quisiera un rollo
kee-S'YEH-ra oon ROHL-yo

. . . in color.
. . . en colores.
. . . en ko-LO-rehs.

. . . black and white.
. . . blanco y negro.
. . . BLAHN-ko ee NEH-gro.

. . . a movie film.
. . . una película.
. . . OO-na peh-LEE-koo-la.

For this camera.
Para esta cámara.
PA-ra ESS-ta KA-ma-ra.

This is to be developed.
Esto es para revelar.
ESS-to ess PA-ra reh-veh-LAR.

How much per print?
¿Cuánto cuesta cada fotografía?
¿KWAHN-to KWEHS-ta KA-da fo-toh-gra-FEE-ya?

Two of each.
Dos de cada una.
dohs deh KA-da OO-na.

An enlargement.
Una ampliación.
OO-na ahm-plee-ya-
S'YOHN.

About this size.
Más o menos de este tamaño.
mahs oh MEH-nohs deh ESS-teh ta-MAHN-yo.

When will they be ready?
¿Cuándo estarán listas?
¿KWAHN-do ess-ta-RAHN LEES-tahs?

May I take a photograph of you?
¿Puedo tomar una foto de Ud.?
¿PWEH-doh toh-MAR OO-na FO-toh deh oo-STED?

Stand here.
Párese acquí.
PA-reh-seh ah-KEE.

Don't move.
No se mueva.
no seh MWEH-va.

Smile.
Sonría.
sohn-REE-ya.

That's it.
Así es.
ah-SEE ess.

Will you kindly take one of me?
¿Me quiere sacar una foto a mí?
¿meh K'YEH-reh sa-KAR OO-na FO-toh ah mee?

In front of this.
Delante de esto.
deh-LAHN-teh deh ESS-toh.

You are very kind.
Ud. es muy amable.
oo-STED ess mwee ah-MA-bleh.

May I send you a copy?
¿Le puedo mandar una copia?
¿leh PWEH-doh mahn-DAR OO-na KOHP-ya?

Your name?
¿Su nombre?
¿soo NOHM-breh?

Your address?
¿Su dirección?
¿soo dee-rek-S'YOHN?

A propósito: Asking to take pictures of someone often leads to more general conversation. For this reason the following sections (13, 14, and 15) will be especially interesting to you.

POINT TO THE ANSWER

To make sure you understand the answer to a question about cameras or film, show the following section to the employee of the "tienda de fotografías" so that he or she can select the answer. The sentence in Spanish after the arrow asks him or her to point to the answer.

 Tenga la bondad de indicar aquí abajo su contestación a mi pregunta. Muchísimas gracias.

Venga mañana.
Come tomorrow.

A las _____.
At _____ o'clock.

Vuelva en _____ días.
Come back in _____ days.

Podemos repararlo.
We can repair it.

No podemos repararlo.
We cannot repair it.

No tenemos.
We haven't any.

Puede conseguirlo en _____.
You can get it at _____.

13. Entertainment

This section will show you how to extend and accept invitations, as well as suggest things to do. It also offers some typical conversations for theater or nightclubs and some suitable words of appreciation when you are asked for dinner.

Things to Do

May I invite you . . .
¿Puedo invitarle . . .
¿PWEH-doh een-vee-TAR-leh . . .

. . . to lunch?
. . . a almorzar?
. . . ah ahl-mor-SAR?

. . . to dinner?
. . . a cenar?
. . . ah seh-NAR?

. . . to have a drink?
. . . a tomar algo?
. . . ah toh-MAR AHL-go?

. . . to go for a drive?
. . . a dar una vuelta en auto?
. . . ah dar OO-na VWEL-ta en OW-toh?

. . . to dance?
. . . a bailar?
. . . ah by-LAR?

. . . to play bridge?
. . . a jugar al bridge?
. . . ah hoo-GAR ahl bridge?

. . . to the movies?
. . . al cine?
. . . ahl SEE-neh?

. . . to the theater?
. . . al teatro?
. . . ahl teh-AH-tro?

. . . to play golf?
. . . a jugar golf?
. . . ah hoo-GAR golf?

. . . to play tennis?
. . . a jugar al tenis?
. . . ah hoo-GAR ahl TEH-neess?

Thank you very much.
Muchas gracias.
MOO-chahs GRA-s'yahs.

71

With pleasure.   **I am sorry.**   **I cannot.**
Con mucho gusto Lo siento.   No puedo.
kohn MOO-cho   lo S'YEN-toh.   no PWEH-doh.
  GOO-sto.

I am busy.   **I am tired.**
Estoy ocupado. (m)   Estoy cansado. (m)
ess-TOY oh-koo-PA-doh.   ess-TOY kahn-SA-doh.
Estoy ocupada. (f)   Estoy cansada. (f)
ess-TOY oh-koo-PA-da.   ess-TOY kahn-SA-da.

I'm waiting for someone.
Estoy esperando a alguien.
ess-TOY ess-peh-RAHN-doh ah AHL-g'yen.

I don't feel well.   **Another time, perhaps.**
No me siento bien.   Una otra vez, quizá.
no meh S'YEN-toh b'yen.   OO-na OH-tra vess, kee-
        SA.

Where are we going tomorrow?
¿Adónde vamos mañana?
¿ah-DOHN-deh VA-mohs mahn-YA-na?

Let's go . . .   **. . . take a walk around**
Vamos . . .   **town.**
VA-mohs . . .   . . . a dar una vuelta por la
        ciudad.
        . . . ah dar OO-na VWEL-
        ta por la s'yoo-DAHD.

. . . to the art museum.   **. . . to the central market.**
. . . al museo de arte.   . . . al mercado central.
. . . ahl moo-SEH-oh deh   *. . . ahl mer-KA-doh sen-*
  AR-teh.   *TRAHL.*

. . . to the cathedral.   **. . . to the palace.**
. . . a la catedral.   . . . al palacio.
. . . ah la ka-teh DRAHL.   *. . . ahl pa-LA-s'yo.*

. . . **to the shops.**
. . . a las tiendas.
. . . *ah lahs T'YEN-dahs.*

. . . **to a typical restaurant.**
. . . a un restaurante típico.
. . . *ah oon rest-ow-RAHN-teh TEE-pee-ko.*

. . . **to the park**
. . . al parque.
. . *ahl PAR-keh.*

. . . **to the zoo.**
. . . al zoológico.
. . . *ahl so-oh-LO-hee-ko.*

. . . **to see the national dances.**
. . . a ver los bailes nacionales.
. . . *ah vehr lohs BY-lehs na-s'yo-NA-lehs.*

. . . **to the meeting.**
. . . a la reunión.
. . . *ah la reh-oo-N'YOHN.*

. . . **to the beach.**
. . . a la playa.
. . . *ah la PLA-ya.*

. . . **to the races.**
. . . a las carreras.
. . . *ah lahs ka-RREH-rahs.*

. . . **to the soccer game.**
. . . al partido de fútbol.
. . . *ahl par-TEE-doh deh FOOT-bohl.*

Who's ahead?
¿Quién está ganando?
¿k'yen ess-TA ga-NAHN-doh?

. . . **to a discoteque.**
. . . a una discoteca.
. . . *ah OO-na dees-ko TEH-ka.*

. . . **to the movies.**
. . . al cine.
. . . *ahl SEE-neh.*

. . . **to the bullfight.**
. . . a la corrida de toros.
. . . *ah la ko-RREE-da deh TOH-rohs.*

Bravo!
¡Ole!
¡OH-leh!

A propósito: Bullfighting, popular in the majority of Spanish countries, has its own vocabulary, such as: the team—**cuadrilla;** the pointed darts—**banderillas;** the horsemen—**picadores;** and the main bullfighter—**el matador** ("the one who kills"). All participants are called **toreros.** The word **toreador** is *never* used. Bullfight tickets are sold for the **sombra** (shade) or **sol** (sun) side of the bullring. When you go, be sure to ask for **una entrada de sombra**—"a ticket in the shade."

Theater and Nightclubs

Let's go to the theater.
Vamos al teatro.
VA-mohs ahl teh-AH-tro.

Two seats, please.
Dos localidades, por favor.
dohs lo-ka-lee-DA-dehss, por fa-VOR.

In the orchestra.
En platea.
en pla-TEH-ah.

In the balcony.
En el balcón.
en el bahl-KOHN.

How beautiful she is!
¡Qué bella es!
¡keh BEL-ya ess!

Who is playing the lead?
¿Quién hace el papel principal?
¿k'yen AH-seh el pa-PEL preen-see-PAHL?

When does it start?
¿Cuándo comienza?
¿KWAHN-doh ko-M'YEN-sa?

What do you think of it?
¿Qué le parece?
¿keh leh pa-REH-seh?

It's very good.
Es muy bueno.
ess mwee BWEH-no.

It's great.
Es fantástico.
ess fahn-TAHS-tee-ko.

It's very amusing.
Es muy divertido.
ess mwee dee-vehr-TEE-doh.

Is it over?
¿Terminó?
¿tehr-mee-NO?

Let's go to a nightclub.
Vamos a un cabaret.
VA-mohs ah oon ka-ba-REH.

A table near the dance floor.
Una mesa cerca de la pista.
OO-na MEH-sa SEHR-ka deh la PEES-ta.

Is there a minimum charge?
¿Hay un mínimo?
¿I oon MEE-nee-no?

Shall we stay?
¿Nos quedamos?
¿nohs keh-DA-mohs?

Shall we dance?
¿Bailamos?
¿by-LA-mohs?

Let's leave.
Vámonos.
VA-mo-nohs.

An Invitation to Dinner

Can you come for dinner at our house, Monday at eight?
¿Puede venir a cenar a casa el lunes a las ocho?
¿PWEH-deh veh-NEER ah seh-NAR ah KA-sa el LOO-nehs ah lahs OH-cho?

With pleasure.
Con mucho gusto.
kohn MOO-cho GOO-sto.

If it isn't inconvenient for you.
Si no es mucha molestia para Ud.
See no ess MOO-cha mo-LES-t'ya PA-ra oo-STED.

Very happy to see you.
Mucho gusto en verle.
MOO-cho GOO-sto en VEHR-leh.

Sorry I'm late.
Siento llegar tarde.
S'YEN-toh l'yeh-GAR TAR-deh.

The traffic was terrible.
El transito estaba terrible.
el TRAHN-see-toh ess-TA-ba teh-RREE-bleh.

Make yourself at home.
Está Ud. en su casa.
ess-TA oo-STED en soo KA-sa.

What a beautiful house!
¡Qué casa tan bella!
¿keh KA-sa tahn BEL-ya!

Will you have something
to drink?
¿Quiere algo de beber?
¿K'YEH-reh AHL-go deh
beh-BEHR?

A cigarette?
¿Un cigarillo?
¿oon see-ga-RREEL-yo?

To your health!
¡A su salud!
¡ah soo sa-LOOD!

Dinner is served.
La cena está servida.
la SEH-na ess-TA sehr-
VEE-da.

Will you sit here, please?
¿Quiere sentarse aquí, por favor?
¿K'YEH-reh sen-TAR-seh ah-KEE, por fa-VOR?

What a delicious meal!
¡Qué comida tan deliciosa!
¡keh ko-MEE-da tahn deh-
lee-S'YO-sa!

But have some more!
¡Pero sírvase más!
¡PEH-ro SEER-va-seh
mahs!

We had a wonderful time.
Nos divertimos mucho.
nohs dee-vehr-TEE-mohs MOO-cho.

We must go.
Tenemos que irnos.
teh-NEH-mohs keh EER-
nohs.

What a shame!
¡Qué lástima!
¡keh LAHS-tee-ma!

I'm sorry, but tomorrow . . .
Lo siento, pero mañana . . .
lo s'YEN-toh, PEH-ro mahn-YA-na . . .

We must take the early flight.
debemos tomar el vuelo temprano.
deh-BEH-mos toh-MAR el v'WEH-lo tem-PRA-no.

I'll drive you back.
Yo los llevo en el auto.
yo lohs L'YEH-vo en el OW-toh.

No, please don't bother.
No, por favor, no se moleste.
no, por fa-VOR, no seh mo-LESS-teh.

A thousand thanks for your hospitality.
Mil gracias por su hospitalidad.
Meel GRA-s'yahs por soo ohs-pee-ta-lee-DAHD.

On the contrary!
¡Al contrario!
¡Ahl kohn-TRA-r'yo!

It was a great pleasure for us.
Fue un gran gusto para nosotros.
Fweh oon grahn GOOS-toh PA-ra no-SO-trohs.

Goodbye! Have a good trip!
¡Adios! ¡Buen viaje!
¡ah-d'YOHS! ¡bwen V'YA-heh!

Until soon.
Hasta pronto.
AHS-ta PROHN-toh.

14. Talking to People

Most phrase books are too preoccupied with attending to one's wants and generally "getting along" to pay much attention to what you should say once you meet someone, such as asking people about themselves, their families, and even their opinions about things. Use of the short phrases in this section, both the questions and the answers, can lead to a rewarding conversational breakthrough in Spanish.

Do you live in this city?
¿Vive Ud. en esta ciudad?
¿VEE-veh oo-STED en ESS-ta s'yoo-DAHD?

Where are you from?
¿De dónde es Ud.?
¿deh DOHN-deh ess oo-STED?

I am from Barcelona.
Soy de Barcelona.
soy deh bar-seh-LO-na.

Really?
¿Verdad?
¿vehr-DAHD?

It's a beautiful city.
Es una hermosa ciudad.
ess OO-na ehr-MO-sa s'yoo-DAHD.

I've been there.
He estado allí.
eh ess-TA-doh ahl-YEE.

I would like to go there.
Me gustaría ir allí.
meh goo-sta-REE-ya eer ahl-YEE.

How long have you been here?
¿Hace cuánto tiempo está aquí?
¿AH-seh KWAHN-toh T'YEM-po ess-TA ah-KEE?

For three days.
Hace tres días.
AH-seh trehs DEE-yahs.

Several weeks.
Varias semanas.
VA-r'yahs seh-MA-nahs.

Two months.
Dos meses.
dohs MEH-sehs.

How long will you stay here?
¿Cuánto tiempo va a quedarse aquí?
¿KWAHN-toh T'YEM-po va ah keh-DAR-seh ah-KEE?

I will stay _____.
Me quedaré _____.
meh keh-da-REH _____.

Have you been here before?
¿Ha estado aquí antes?
¿ah ess-TA-doh ah-KEE AHN-tehs?

No, never.
No, nunca.
no, NOON-ka.

Once.
Una vez.
OO-na vess.

Five years ago.
Hace cinco años.
AH-seh SEEN-ko AHN-yohs.

Where are you living?
¿Dónde vive Ud.?
¿DOHN-deh VEE-veh oo-STED?

At what hotel?
¿En qué hotel?
¿en keh o-TEL?

What do you think of Sevilla?
¿Qué le parece Sevilla?
¿keh leh pa-REH-seh seh-VEEL-ya?

I like it very much.
Me gusta mucho.
meh GOO-sta MOO-cho.

It's very interesting.
Es muy interesante.
ess mwee een-teh-reh-SAHN-teh.

The city is beautiful.
La ciudad es hermosa.
la s'yoo-DAHD ess ehr-MO-sa.

The women are very beautiful.
Las mujeres son muy hermosas.
las moo-HEH-rehs son mwee ehr-MO-sahs.

Have you been in Granada?
¿Ha estado Ud. en Granada?
¿ah ess-TA-doh oo-STED en gra-NA-da?

You must go there.
Tiene que ir allá.
T'YEH-neh keh eer ahl-YA.

Are you from the United States?
¿Es Ud. de los Estados Unidos?
¿ess oo-STED deh lohs ess-TA-dohs oo-NEE-dohs?

Yes, I am from San Francisco.
Sí, soy de San Francisco.
see, soy deh sahn frahn-SEES-ko.

I speak a little Spanish.
Hablo un poquito de español.
AH-blo oon po-KEE-toh deh ess-pahn-YOHL.

But you have a good accent.
Pero Ud. tiene un buen acento.
PEH-ro oo-STED T'YEH-neh oon bwehn ah-SEN-toh.

You are very kind.
Ud. es muy amable.
oo-STED ess mwee ah-MA-bleh.

Have you been in the United States?
¿Ha estado en los Estados Unidos?
¿ah ess-TA-doh en lohs ess-TA-dohs oo-NEE-dohs?

Where have you been?
¿Dónde ha estado?
¿DOHN-deh ah ess-TA-doh?

What do you think of _____?
¿Qué piensa de _____?
¿keh P'YEN-sa deh _____?

Do you like _____?   **I like _____.**
¿Le gusta _____?   Me gusta _____.
¿leh GOO-sta _____?   *meh GOO-sta _____.*

When people ask your opinion about something, you will find the following comments most helpful.

Very interesting.
Muy interesante.
mwee een-teh-reh-SAHN-teh.

Not bad.
No está mal.
no ess-TA mahl.

Magnificent.
Magnífico.
mahg-NEE-fee-ko.

Wonderful.
Maravilloso.
ma-ra-veel-YO-so.

Sometimes.
Algunas veces.
ahl-GOO-nahs VEH-sehs.

Often.
A menudo.
ah meh-NOO-doh.

Never.
Nunca.
NOON-ka.

It seems to me that . . .
Me parece que . . .
meh pa-REH-seh keh . . .

In any case . . .
En todo caso . . .
en TOH-doh KA-so . . .

It's a shame!
¡Es una lástima!
¡ess OO-na LAHS-tee-ma!

I agree with you.
Estoy de acuerdo.
ess-TOY deh ah-KWER-doh.

I don't know.
No sé.
no seh.

I have forgotten.
He olvidado.
eh ohl-vee-DA-doh.

Is it possible?
¿Es posible?
¿ess po-SEE-bleh?

That's true.
Es verdad.
ess vehr-DAHD.

You must come to see us.
Debe Ud. venir a vernos.
DEH-beh oo-STED veh-NEER ah VEHR-nohs.

At our house.
En nuestra casa.
en NWESS-tra KA-sa.

It would be a great pleasure.
Sería un gran placer.
seh-REE-ya oon grahn pla-SEHR.

Are you married?

¿Es Ud. casado? (m)   ¿Es Ud. casada? (f)
¿ess oo-STED ka-SA-doh?   *¿ess oo-STED ka-SA-da?*

I am not married.   **I am married.**
Soy soltero. (m)   Soy casado. (m)
soy sohl-TEH-ro.   *soy ka-SA-doh.*
Soy soltera. (f)   Soy casada. (f)
soy sohl-TEH-ra.   *soy ka-SA-da.*

Is your wife (husband) here?
¿Está aquí su esposa (esposo)?
¿ess-TA ah-KEE soo ess-PO-sa (ess-PO-so)?

Yes, over there.   **Do you have children?**
Sí, allá.   ¿Tiene niños?
see, ahl-YA.   *¿T'YEH-neh NEEN-yohs?*

No, I haven't.   **Yes, I have.**
No, no tengo.   Sí, tengo.
No, no TEN-go.   *see, TEN-go*

How many boys?
¿Cuántos niños?
¿KWAHN-tohs NEEN-yohs?

How many girls?
¿Cuántas niñas?
¿KWAHN-tahs NEEN-yahs?

How old are they?
¿Cuántos años tienen?
¿KWAHN-tohs AHN-yohs t'YEH-nen?

My son is seven years old.
Mi hijo tiene siete años.
mee EE-ho T'YEH-neh S'YEH-teh AHN-yohs.

My daughter is ten years old.
Mi hija tiene diez años.
mee EE-ha T'YEH-neh d'yess AHN-yohs.

What cute children!
¡Qué niños tan monos!
¡keh NEEN-yohs tahn MO-nohs!

This is my . . .	**. . . mother.**	**. . . sister.**
Ésta es mi . . .	. . . madre.	. . . hermana.
ESS-ta ess mee . . .	*. . . MA-dreh.*	*. . . ehr-MA-na.*

. . . wife.	**. . . daughter.**
. . . esposa.	. . . hija.
. . . es-PO-sa.	*. . . EE-ha.*

. . . daughter-in-law.	**. . . granddaughter.**
. . . nuera.	. . . nieta.
. . . NWEH-ra.	*. . . N'YEH-ta.*

This is my . . .	**. . . father.**	**. . . brother.**
Éste es mi . . .	. . . padre.	. . . hermano.
ESS-teh ess mee . . .	*. . . PA-dreh.*	*. . . ehr-MA-no.*

. . . husband.	**. . . son.**
. . . esposo.	. . . hijo.
. . . ess-PO-so.	*. . . EE-ho.*

. . . son-in-law.	**. . . grandson.**
. . . yerno.	. . . nieto.
. . . YEHR-no.	*. . . N'YEH-to.*

For "your," "his," or "her" use **su** in place of **mi**—"my."

Do you know	**that man?**	**. . . that lady?**
Conoce Ud. a	ese hombre?	. . . esa señora?
ko-NO-seh oo-STED ah . . .	*. . . ESS-seh OHM-breh?*	*. . . ESS-sa sen-YO-ra?*

. . . Mrs. Martin?
. . . la señora de Martín?
. . . la sen-YO-ra deh mar-TEEN?

He is . . .   **. . . a writer.**
Él es . . .   . . . escritor.
el ess . . .   . . . *ess-kree-TOR.*

. . . a businessman.
. . . hombre de negocios.
. . . *OHM-breh deh neh-GO-s'yohs.*

. . . a lawyer.   **. . . a**   **. . . a doctor.**
. . . abogado.   **manufacturer.**   . . . doctor.
. . . *ah-bo-GA-*   . . . fabricante.   . . . *dohk-TOR.*
    doh.   . . . *fa-bree-*
                           KAHN-teh.

. . . a banker.   **. . . a military**   **. . . a painter.**
. . . banquero.   **man.**   . . . pintor.
. . . *bahn-KEH-*   . . . militar.   . . . *peen-TOR.*
    ro.   . . . *mee-lee-TAR.*

. . . a professor.   **. . . a politician.**   **. . . an actor.**
. . . profesor.   . . . político.   . . . actor.
. . . *pro-feh-SOR.*   . . . *po-LEE-teek-*   . . . *ahk-TOR.*
                             ko.

. . . a member of the government.
. . . miembro del gobierno.
. . . *M'YEM-bro del go-B'YEHR-no.*

She is . . .   **. . . a writer.**
Ella es . . .   . . . escritora.
EL-ya ess . . .   . . . *ess-kree-TOH-ra*

. . . a singer.   **. . . an actress.**   **. . . a teacher.**
. . . cantante.   . . . actriz.   . . . maestra.
. . . *kahn-TAHN-*   . . . *ahk-TREESS.*   . . . *ma-ESS-tra.*
    teh.

And for other masculine endings in *-or,* add *-a* for a woman.

I don't know.   **I'll find out.**
No sé.   Averiguaré.
no seh.   *ah-veh-ree-gwa-REH.*

He is Spanish.
Él es español.
el ess ess-pahn-YOHL.

She is Spanish.
Ella es española.
EL-ya ess ess-pahn-YO-la.

He is Mexican.
Él es mexicano.
el ess meh-hee-KA-no.

She is Mexican.
Ella es mexicana.
EL-ya ess meh-hee-KA-na.

He is North American.
(from the U.S.)
Él es norteamericano.
*el ess nor-teh-ah-meh-ree-
KA-no.*

She is North American.
Ella es norteamericana.
*EL-ya ess nor-teh-ah-meh-
ree-KA-na.*

He is English.
El es inglés.
el ess een-GLEHSS.

She is English.
Ella es inglesa.
EL-ya ess een-GLEH-sa.

A propósito: For nationalities of Spanish-speaking and other important countries, see the dictionary section.

He is very nice.
Él es muy simpático.
*el ess mwee seem-PA-tee-
ko.*

She is very nice.
Ella es muy simpática.
*El-ya ess mwee seem-PA-
tee-ka.*

She is very pretty.
Ella es muy bonita.
*EL-ya ess mwee bo-NEE-
ta.*

He (she) is very intelligent.
Él (ella) es muy inteligente.
*el (EL-ya) ess mwee een-
teh-lee-HEN-teh.*

He (she) is very capable.
Él (ella) es muy capaz.
*el (EL-ya) ess mwee ka-
PAHS.*

Here is my address.
Aquí está mi dirección.
*ah-KEE ess-TA mee dee-
rek-S'YOHN.*

What is your address?
¿Cuál es su dirreción?
¿kwahl ess soo dee-rek-SYOHN?

Here is my telephone number.
Aquí está mi número de teléfono.
ah-KEE ess-TA mee NOO-meh-ro-deh teh-LEH-fo-no.

What is your telephone number?
¿Cuál es su número de teléfono?
¿kwahl ess soo NOO-meh-ro deh-teh-LEH-fo-no?

May I call you?
¿Puedo llamarle?
¿PWEH-doh l'ya-MAR-leh?

When?
¿Cuándo?
¿KWAHN-doh?

Tomorrow morning.
Mañana por la mañana.
mahn-YA-na por la mahn-YA-na.

Early.
Temprano.
tem-PRA-no.

In the afternoon.
Por la tarde.
por la TAR-deh.

What is your first name?
¿Cuál es su primer nombre?
¿kwahl ess soo pree-MEHR NOHM-breh?

Mine is Richard.
El mío es Ricardo.
el MEE-yo ess ree-KAR-do.

You dance very well.
Ud. baila muy bien.
oo-STED BY-la mwee b'yen.

You sing very well.
Ud. canta muy bien.
oo-STED KAHN-ta mwee b'yen.

What a pretty dress!
¡Qué vestido tan bonito!
¡keh ves-TEE-doh tahn bo-NEE-toh!

I have a surprise for you.
Tengo una sorpresa para Ud.
TEN-go OO-na sor-PREH-sa PA-ra oo-STED.

Do you like it?
¿Le gusta?
¿leh GOOS-ta?

Can we see each other again?
¿Podemos volver a vernos?
¿po-DEH-mohs vohl-VEHR ah VEHR-nohs?

When?	**Where?**	**Why?**
¿Cuándo?	¿Dónde?	¿Por qué?
¿KWAHN-doh?	*¿DOHN-deh?*	*¿por keh?*

Are you angry?
¿Está enojado? (to a man)
¿ess-TA eh-no-HA-doh?

¿Está enojada? (to a woman)
¿ess-TA eh-no-HA-da?

What's the matter?
¿Qué le pasa?
¿keh leh PA-sa?

I'm very sorry.
Lo siento mucho.
lo s'YEN-toh MOO-cho.

Where are you going?
¿A dónde va?
¿ah DOHN-deh va?

Let's go together.
Vamos juntos.
VA-mohs HOON-tohs.

You are intelligent.
Ud. es inteligente.
oo-STED ess een-teh-lee-HEN-teh.

You are very beautiful.
Ud. es muy hermosa. (f)
oo-STED ess mwee ehr-MO-sa.

You are very nice.
Ud. es muy simpática. (f)
oo-STED ess mwee seem-PA-tee-ka.

Will you give me your photograph?
¿Me da una foto de Ud.?
¿meh da OO-na FO-toh deh oo-STED?

Will you write to me?
¿Me escribirá?
¿meh ess-kree-bee-RA?

Don't forget.
No se olvide.
no seh ohl-VEE-deh.

I like you very much.
Yo te quiero mucho.
yo teh K'YEH-ro MOO-cho.

Really?
¿De verdad?
¿deh vehr-DAHD?

Do you like me too?
¿Me quieres a mí también?
¿meh K'YEH-rehs ah mee tahm-B'YEN?

I love you.
Te quiero.
teh K'YEH-ro.

A propósito: In the last sentences we have used the familiar form for "you," both in the verb and the pronoun, since the tone of the conversation implies some degree of familiarity.

"To like," "to love," and "to want" are all expressed by the same verb—**querer**.

15. Words That Show You Are "With It"

There are certain words that Spanish-speaking people use constantly but that do not always have an exact equivalent in English. To use them at the right time will cause Spanish people to consider that you have good manners and are familiar with the most frequent Spanish conversational phrases—in other words, that you are "with it." The Spanish is given first, just as you will hear these expressions occur in everyday conversation.

We have divided these words into two groups; the first one is composed of selected polite expressions:

¡Buen Viaje!
¡bwehn V'YA-heh!
Have a good trip!

¡Que se divierta!
¡keh seh dee-V'YEHR-ta!
Enjoy yourself!

¡Que lo pase bien!
¡Keh lo PA-seh b'yen!
Have a nice time!

¡Felicitaciones!
¡feh-lee-see-ta-S'YO-nehs!
Congratulations!

Mis saludos a . . .
mees sa-LOO-dohs ah . . .
My regards to . . .

¡A su salud!
¡ah soo sa-LOOD!
To your health!

When you see someone eating you say:

¡Buen provecho!
¡bwehn pro-VEH-cho!
Good benefit!

or

¡Que aproveche!
¡keh ah-pro-VEH-cheh!
May you enjoy it!

When someone sneezes you say:

¡Salud! (or) **¡Jesús!**
¡sa-LOOD! ¡heh-SOOS!
Health! Jesus!

When someone leaves the room or passes in front of someone, he says:

Con permiso.
kohn pehr-MEE-so.
With permission.

To which the answer is:

¿Cómo no?
¿KO-mo no?
How (why) not?

To a visitor to your house you say:

¡Está en su casa!
¡ess-TA en soo KA-sa!
Make yourself at home! (You are in your house!)

To someone who admires something of yours:

Es suyo. or **Es suya.**
ess SOO-yo. ess SOO-ya
It is yours.

(Use **suyo** if the thing is masculine, **suya** if it is feminine.)

A propósito: In general be careful about admiring small objects, because the reply **Es suyo** sometimes means that it will literally be given to you. It is better to admire the home or the garden, and the reply **Es suyo** or **Está a su disposición** means that it is yours to enjoy (but not to take away).

As the following phrases permeate conversation, it will interest you to know what they mean, as well as to learn to use them as helpful conversational stopgaps. The translations are quite free as these expressions are very idiomatic.

¡Claro!	**Pues . . .**	**Entonces . . .**
¡KLA-ro!	*pwehss . . .*	*en-TOHN-sehs . . .*
Of course!	So . . .	Then, so . . .

Bueno . . .
BWEH-no . . .
Well . . .

No me diga.
no meh DEE-ga.
You don't say . . .

¿Qué pasa?
¿keh PA-sa?
What's
  happening?

¿Qué tal?
¿keh tahl?
How goes it?

Así, así.
ah-SEE, ah-SEE.
So, so.

¿No es verdad?
*¿no ess vehr-
  DAHD?*
Isn't it so?

¡Qué raro!
¡keh RA-ro!
How strange!

¡Qué va!
¡keh va!
Not at all!

No se preocupe.
*no seh preh-oh-
  KOO-peh.*
Don't worry.

Vamos a ver.
VA-mohs ah vehr.
Let's see.

No es nada.
no ess NA-da.
It's nothing.

No importa.
no eem-POR-ta.
It doesn't matter.

Lo mismo da.
lo MEES-mo da.
It's all the same.

No vale la pena.
no VA-leh la PEH-na.
It isn't worthwhile.

Más o menos.
*mahs oh MEH-
  nohs.*
More or less.

En todo caso . . .
*en TO-doh KA-
  so . . .*
In any case . . .

Cualquier cosa.
*kwahl-K'YEHR
  KO-sa.*
Anything.

¡Fíjese!
¡FEE-heh-seh!
Just imagine!

¡Ni hablar!
¡nee ah-BLAR!
Don't mention it!

¿Qué hay?
¿keh I?
What's up?

Parece mentira.
pa-REH-seh men-TEE-ra.
It seems a lie (impossible).

¿Cómo dice?
¿KO-mo DEE-seh?
What's that? or How's
  that?

¡Caramba!
¡ka-RAHM-ba!
Good Heavens! Well, really! For Heaven's sake!

No faltaba más.
no fahl-TA-ba mahs.
That's all we needed.

¡Eso es!
¡ES-so ess!
That's it!

Me parece que . . .
Meh pa-reh-seh keh . . .
It seems to me that . . .

¡Ole!
¡OH-le! or oh-LAY
(A shout of approval for a
    dancer, bullfighter, or
    anything outstanding.)

¡Qué lindo!
Keh LEEN-doh!
How beautiful! (When applied to the feminine gender,
change the final "o" to "a".)

¡Es eso verdad?
Ess ESS-so vehr-DAHD?
Is that true?

¡Qué mala suerte!
Keh MA-la SWEHR-teh.
What bad luck!

¡Dios mío!
¡d'yohs MEE-yo!
My God! (Great heavens!)

¡Ave María!
¡AH-veh ma-REE-ya!
Hail Mary! (Great
    heavens!)

¡Hombre!	**¡Mujer!**	**¡Chico!**	**¡Chica!**
¡OHM-breh!	*¡moo-HEHR!*	*¡CHEE-ko!*	*¡CHEE-ka!*
Man!	Woman!	Boy!	Girl!

A propósito: The last four words are used colloquially to
give emphasis or punctuation to what you are saying.
¡Hombre! is the most widely used, sometimes even by
women talking to each other.

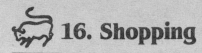 **16. Shopping**

Shops in Spain and Latin America still tend to be specialized although there exist chains of general stores and even the supermarket—**supermercado**.

Names of Shops

Where can one find . . .
¿Dónde se puede encontrar . . .
¿DOHN-deh seh PWEH-deh en-koh'n-TRAR . . .

. . . a department store?
. . . una tienda de departamentos?
. . . OO-na T'YEN-da deh deh-par-ta-MEN-tohs?

. . . a dress shop?
. . . una tienda de vestidos?
. . . OO-na T'Yen-da deh ves-TEE-dohs?

. . . a hat shop?
. . . una sombrerería?
. . . OO-na som-breh-reh-REE-ya?

. . . a perfume shop?
. . . una perfumería?
. . . OO-na per-foo-meh-REE-ya?

. . . a jewelry shop?
. . . una joyería?
. . . OO-na ho-yeh-REE-ya?

. . . a drugstore?
. . . una farmacia?
. . . OO-na far-MA-s'ya?

. . . a book shop?
. . . una librería?
. . . OO-na lee-breh-REE-ya?

. . . a toy shop?
. . . una juguetería?
. . . OO-na hoo-geh-teh-REE-ya?

. . . an antique shop?
. . . una tienda de antigüedades?
. . . OO-na T'YEN-da deh ahn-tee-gweh-DA-dehs?

. . . **a shoe store?**
. . . una zapatería?
. . . *OO-na sa-pa-teh-REE-ya?*

. . . **a flower shop?**
. . . una floristería?
. . . *OO-na flo-rees-teh-REE-ya?*

. . . **a camera shop?**
. . . una tienda para artículos de fotografía?
. . . *OO-na T'YEN-da PA-ra ar-TEE-koo-lohs de fo-toh-gra-FEE-ya?*

. . . **a tobacco shop?**
. . . una tabaquería?
. . . *OO-na ta-ba-keh-REE-ya?*

. . . **a beauty shop?**
. . . un salón de belleza?
. . . *oon sa-LOHN deh behl-YEH-sa?*

. . . **a barber shop?**
. . . una barbería?
. . . *OO-na bar-beh-REE-ya?*

. . . **a grocery store!**
. . . una casa de comestibles?
. . . *OO-na KA-sa deh ko-mehs-TEE-blehs?*

. . . **a market?**
. . . un mercado?
. . . *oon mehr-KA-doh?*

A propósito: A mercado is also a general market place and, in Latin America, is often held in the plaza of small towns and villages on certain days each week.

General Shopping Vocabulary

May I help you?
¿En qué puedo servirle?
¿en keh PWEH-doh sehr-
  VEER-leh?

What do you wish?
¿Qué desea?
¿keh deh-SEH-ah?

I would like to buy . . .
Me gustaría comprar . . .
meh goo-sta-REE-ya kohm-
  PRAR . . .

. . . a gift for my husband.
. . . un regalo para mi
esposo.
. . . oon reh-GA-lo PA-ra
  mee es-PO-so.

. . . a gift for my wife.
. . . un regalo para mi señora.
. . . oon reh-GA-lo PA-ra mee sen-YO-ra.

. . . something for a man.
. . . algo para un hombre.
. . . AHL-go PA-ra oon OHM-breh.

. . . something for a lady.
. . . algo para una dama.
. . . AHL-go PA-ra OO-na DA-ma.

Nothing for the moment.
Nada por el momento.
NA-da por el mo-MEN-toh.

I'm just looking around.
Estoy mirando solamente.
es-TOY mee-RAHN-doh so-la-MEN-teh.

I'll be back later.
Regreso más tarde.
reh-GREH-so mahs TAR-deh.

I like this.
Me gusta esto.
meh GOO-sta ESS-toh.

. . . that.
. . . eso.
. . . ES-so.

How much is it?
¿Cuánto es?
¿KWAHN-toh ess?

Show me another.
Muéstreme otro.
MWEHS-treh-meh OH-tro.

Something less expensive.
Algo menos caro.
AHL-go MEH-nohs KA-ro.

Do you like this?
¿Le gusta esto?
¿leh GOO-sta ESS-toh?

Is it handmade?
¿Está hecho a mano?
¿ess-TA EH-cho ah MA-no?

. . . hand embroidered?
. . .bordado a mano?
. . . bor-DA-doh ah MA-no?

May I try it on?
¿Puedo probármelo?
¿PWEH-doh pro-BAR-meh-lo?

That suits you very well.
Le queda muy bien.
leh KEH-da mwee b'yen.

Can you alter it?
¿Puede arreglarlo?
¿PWEH-deh ah-rreh-GLAR-lo?

Good. I'll take it.
Bien. Lo tomo.
b'yen, lo TOH-mo.

Will you wrap it?
¿Quiere envolverlo?
¿K'YEH-reh en-vohl-VEHR-lo?

Can you send it to this address?
¿Puede mandarlo a esta dirección?
¿PWEH-deh mahn-DAR-lo ah ESS-ta dee-rek-S'YOHN?

Can one pay by check?
¿Se puede pagar con cheque?
¿seh PWEH-deh pa-GAR kohn CHEH-keh?

A receipt, please.
Un recibo, por favor.
oon reh-SEE-bo, por fa-VOR.

The change, please.
El cambio, por favor.
el KAHM-b'yo, por fa-VOR.

Bargains   **Sale**
Gangas   Venta
GAHN-gahs   *VEN-ta*

POINT TO THE ANSWER

To make sure you understand the answer to a question you have asked about shopping, show the following section to the salesperson so that he or she can select the answer. The sentence in Spanish after the arrow asks him or her to point to the answer.

 Tenga la bondad de indicar aquí abajo su contestación a mi pregunta. Muchísimas gracias.

No tenemos.
We haven't any.

Es todo lo que tenemos de esta clase.
That's all we have of this type.

No tenemos más grandes.   **No tenemos más chicos.**
We haven't any larger.   We haven't any smaller.

No tenemos servicio de entrega.
We don't have delivery service.

Podemos mandarlo a una dirección en los Estados Unidos.
We can send it to an address in the United States.

¿Cuál es su dirección?
What is your address?

No aceptamos cheques personales.
We don't accept personal checks.

Aceptamos cheques viajeros.
We accept travelers checks.

Clothes

a blouse
una blusa
OO-na BLOO-sa

a skirt
una falda
OO-na FAHL-da

A (woman's) suit
un taller
oon tahl-YEHR.

a coat
un abrigo
oon ah-BREE-go

a hat
un sombrero
oon sohm-BREH-ro

a scarf
una bufanda
OO-na boo-FAHN-da

a handbag
una cartera
OO-na kar-TEH-ra

gloves
guantes
GWAHN-tehs

a dress (or) **suit**
un vestido
oon vess-TEE-doh

a shirt
una camisa
OO-na ka-MEE-sa

pants
pantalones
pahn-ta-LO-nehs

a (man's) suit
un traje
oon TRA-heh

a jacket
una chaqueta
OO-na cha-KEH-ta

socks
calcetines
kahl-seh-TEE-nehs

a tie
una corbata
OO-na kor-BA-ta

an undershirt
una camiseta
OO-na ka-mee-SEH-ta

undershorts
calzoncillos
kahl-sohn-SEEL-yohs

stockings
medias
MEHD-yahs

a slip
un refajo
oon reh-FA-ho

a brassiere
un sostén
oon sohs-TEN

panties
pantaletas
pahn-ta-LEH-tahs

pajamas
piyama
pee-YA-ma

a nightgown
una camisa de
   dormir
*OO-na ka-MEE-
   sa deh dor-
   MEER*

a bathrobe
una bata
OO-na BA-ta

a swimsuit
un traje de baño
oon TRA-heh deh BAHN-yo

a raincoat
un impermeable
oon eem-pehr-meh-AH-bleh

boots
botas
BO-tahs

sandals
sandalias
sahn-DA-l'yahs

shoes
zapatos
sa-PA-tohs

slippers
chinelas
chee-NEH-lahs

Sizes—Colors—Materials

What size?
¿Qué tamaño?
*¿Keh ta-MAHN-
   yo?*

small
pequeño
peh-KEN-yo ·

medium
medio
MEH-d'yo

large
grande
GRAHN-deh

extra large
extra grande
EX-tra GRAHN-deh

larger
más grande
mahs GRAHN-deh

smaller
más pequeño
mahs peh-KEN-yo

wider
más ancho
mahs AHN-cho

narrower	**longer**	**shorter**
más angosto	más largo	más corto
mahs ahn-GOHS-	*mahs LAR-go*	*mahs KOR-toh*
toh		

What color?	**red**	**blue**	**yellow**
¿De qué color?	rojo	azul	amarillo
¿deh keh ko-	*RO-ho*	*ah-SOOL*	*ah-ma-*
LOR?			*REEL-yo*

orange	**green**	**purple**
anaranjado	verde	violeta
ah-na-rahn-HA-	*VEHR-deh*	*v'yo-LEH-ta*
doh		

brown	**gray**	**tan**
marrón	gris	crema
ma-RROHN	*greess*	*KREH-ma*

black	**white**	**darker**	**lighter**
negro	blanco	más oscuro	más claro
NEH-gro	*BLAHN-ko*	*mahs ohs-*	*mahs KLA-ro*
		KOO-ro	

Is it silk?	**linen**	**velvet**	**wool**
¿Es de seda?	lino	terciopelo	lana
¿ess deh	*LEE-no*	*tehr-s'yo-*	*LA-na*
SEH-da?		*PEH-lo*	

cotton	**lace**	**nylon**	**dacron**
algodón	encaje	nilón	dacrón
ahl-go-	*en-KA-heh*	*nee-LOHN*	*da-KROHN*
DOHN			

leather	**suede**
cuero	gamuza
KWEH-ro	*go-MOO-sa*

kid	**plastic**	**fur**
cabretilla	plástico	piel
ka-breh-TEEL-ya	*PLAHS-tee-ko*	*p'yehl*

What kind of fur?	**fox**	**beaver**
¿Qué clase de	zorro	castor
piel?	*SO-rro*	*kahs-TOR*
¿keh KLA-seh deh		
p'yehl?		

seal	**mink**	**chinchilla**
foca	visón	chinchilla
FO-ka	*vee-SOHN*	*cheen-CHEEL-ya*

Newsstand

I would like . . .   **. . . a guidebook.**
Me gustaría . . .   . . . una guía.
meh goo-sta-REE-ya . . .   *. . . OO-na GHEE-ya.*

. . . a map of the city.
. . . un mapa de la ciudad.
. . . oon MA-pa deh la s'yoo-DAHD.

. . . postcards.
. . . tarjetas postales.
. . . tar-HEH-tahs pos-TA-lehs

. . . this paper.   **. . . that magazine.**
. . . este periódico.   . . . esa revista.
. . . ESS-teh peh-R'YO-dee- *. . . ES-sa reh-VEESS-ta.*
ko.

. . . A newspaper in English.
. . . un periódico en inglés.
. . . oon peh-R'YO-dee-ko en een-GLEHS.

Tobacco Shop

Have you American cigarettes?
¿Tiene cigarrillos americanos?
¿T'YEH-neh see-gar-REEL-yohs ah-meh-ree-KA-nohs?

cigars	a pipe	tobacco
tabacos	una pipa	picadura
ta-BA-kohs	*OO-na PEE-pa*	*pee-ka-DOO-ra*

matches	a lighter	lighter fluid
fósforos	encendedor	bencina
FOHS-fo-rohs	*en-sen-deh-DOHR*	*ben-SEE-na*

Drugstore

a toothbrush
un cepillo de dientes
oon seh-PEEL-yo deh D'YEN-tehs

toothpaste
pasta de dientes
PAHS-ta deh D'YEN-tehs

a safety razor
una navaja de seguridad
OO-na na-VA-ha deh seh-goo-ree-DAHD

razor blades
hojillas
oh-HEEL-yahs

shaving cream
crema de afeitar
KREH-ma deh ah-fay-TAR

cologne
colonia
ko-LO-n'ya

an electric razor
una máquina de afeitar
OO-na MA-kee-na deh ah-fay-TAR

a hairbrush
un cepillo
oon-seh-PEEL-yo

a comb
un peine
oon PAY-neh

aspirin
aspirina
ahs-pee-REE-na

iodine
yodo
YO-doh

scissors
tijeras
tee-HEH-rahs

a nail file
una lima de uñas
OO-na LEE-ma deh OON-yahs

antiseptic
antiséptico
ahn-tee-SEP-tee-ko

adhesive tape
esparadrapo
ess-pa-ra-DRA-po

coughdrops
pastillas para la tos
pahs-TEEL-yahs PA-ra la tohs

sunglasses
lentes de sol
LEN-tehs deh sohl

Cosmetics

make-up base
base
BAH-seh

powder
polvo
POHL-vo

lipstick
pintura de labio
peen-TOO-ra deh LA-b'yo

eye shadow
sombra
SOHM-bra

nail polish
pintura de uñas
peen-TOO-ra deh OON-yahs

eyebrow pencil
lápiz para las cejas
LA-pees PA-ra lahs SEH-hahs

cleansing cream
crema limpiadora
KREH-ma leem-p'ya-DOH-ra

cotton
algodón
ahl-go-DOHN

bobby pins
ganchitos
gahn-CHEE-tohs

hair spray
laca
LA-ka

shampoo
shampú
shahm-POO

perfume
perfume
pehr-FOO-meh

That smells good, doesn't it?
Eso huele bien, ¿verdad?
EH-so WEH-leh b'yen, ¿vehr-DAHD?

Hairdresser

shampoo and set
lavar y peinar
la-VAR ee pay-NAHR

the part
la raya
la RA-ya

like this
así
ah-SEE

a manicure
una manicura
OO-na ma-nee-KOO-rah

a pedicure
una pedicura
OO-na peh-dee-KOO-rah

a tint
un tinte
oon TEEN-teh

lighter
más claro
mahs KLA-ro

darker
más oscuro
mahs ohs-KOO-ro

Barber

a shave
afeitar
ah-fay-TAR

a haircut
un corte de pelo
oon KOR-teh deh PEH-lo

a massage
un masaje
oon ma-SA-heh

Use scissors.
Use tijeras.
OO-seh tee-HEH-rahs.

shorter
más corto
mahs KOR-toh

not too short
no demasiado corto
no deh-mahs-YA-doh KOR-toh

on top
arriba
ah-REE-ba

in back
atrás
ah-TRAHS

the sides
los lados
lohs LA-dohs

That's fine.
Está bien.
ess-TA b'yen.

Food Market

I would like . . .
Me gustaría . . .
meh goo-sta-REE-ya . . .

a dozen
una docena
OO-na doh-SEH-na

of this
de esto
deh ESS-toh

of that
de eso
deh ES-so.

I want five.
Quiero cinco.
K'YEH-ro SEEN-ko.

Is this fresh?
¿Está fresco esto?
¿ess-TA FRES-ko ESS-toh?

What is this?
¿Qué es esto?
¿keh ess ESS-toh?

Three cans of this.
Tres latas de esto.
tres LA-tahs deh ESS-toh.

How much per kilo?
¿Cuánto cuesta el kilo?
¿KWAHN-toh KWESS-ta el KEE-lo?

Can one buy wine here?
¿Se puede comprar vino aquí?
¿seh PWEH-deh kohm-PRAR VEE-no ah-KEE?

Sherry.
Vino de Jerez.
VEE-no deh heh-REIIS.

Put it in a bag, please.
Póngalo en una bolsa, por favor.
POHN-ga-lo en OO-na BOHL-sa, por fa-VOR.

A propósito: Weight is measured by the kilo (kilogram—**kilogramo**) rather than by the pound. One kilo is equivalent to 2.2 pounds.

Jewelry

I would like . . .
Quisiera . . .
kee-S'YEH-ra . . .

. . . a watch.
. . . un reloj.
. . . oon reh-LO.

. . . a ring.
. . . un anillo.
. . . oon ah-NEEL-yo.

. . . a necklace.
. . . un collar.
. . . oon kohl-YAR.

. . . a bracelet.
. . . un brazalete.
. . . oon bra-sa-LEH-teh.

. . . earrings.
. . . unos pendientes.
. . . OO-nos pen-D'YEN-tehs.

Is this gold? . . . **platinum?** . . . **silver?**
¿Es esto oro? . . . platino? . . . plata?
¿ess ESS-toh OH- . . . *pla-TEE-no?* . . . *PLA-ta?*
ro?

Is it solid or gold-plated? **a diamond**
¿Es macizo o dorado? un brillante
¿ess ma-SEE-so oh do-RA- *oon breel-YAHN-teh*
doh?

pearls **a ruby** **a sapphire**
perlas un rubí un zafiro
PEHR-lahs *oon roo-BEE* *oon sa-FEE-ro*

an amethyst **an emerald** **an aquamarine**
una amatista una esmeralda una aguamarina
OO-na ah-ma- *OO-na es-meh-* *OO-na ah-gwa-*
TEESS-ta *RAHL-da* *ma-REE-na*

Antiques

What period is this? **It's beautiful.**
¿De qué período es esto? Es bello.
¿deh keh peh-REE-oh-doh *ess BEL-yo.*
ess ESS-toh?

But very expensive. **How much is . . .**
Pero muy caro. ¿Cuánto cuesta . . .
PEH-ro mwee KA-ro. *¿KWAHN-toh KWESS-*
ta . . .

. . . **this book?** . . . **this picture?**
. . . este libro? . . . este cuadro?
. . . *ESS-teh LEE-bro?* . . . *ESS-teh KWA-dro?*

. . . **this map?** . . . **this frame?**
. . . este mapa? . . . este marco?
. . . *ESS-teh MA-pa?* . . . *ESS-teh MAR-ko?*

. . . this piece of furniture?
. . . este mueble?
. . . *ESS-teh MWEH-bleh?*

Is it an antique?
¿Es una antigüedad?
¿ess OO-na ahn-tee-gweh-DAHD?

Can you ship it?
¿Puede mandarlo?
¿PWEH-deh mahn-DAR-lo?

To this address.
A esta dirección.
ah ESS-ta dee-rek-S'YOHN.

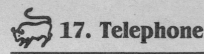 # 17. Telephone

Talking on the telephone is an excellent test of your ability to communicate in Spanish because you can't see the person you are talking to or use gestures to help get across your meaning. When asking for someone, simply say his name and add **por favor**. If you say the number instead of dialing it, say the numbers in pairs. 606642 would be 60-66-42: **sesenta-sesenta y seis-cuarenta y dos**.

Where is the telephone?
¿Dónde está el teléfono?
¿DOHN-deh ess-TA el teh-LEH-fo-no?

The telephone operator.
La telefonista.
la teh-leh-fo-NEES-ta.

Hello!
¡Hola!   *or*   A ver.   *or*
¡OH-la!   ah vehr.

¿Dígame! *or* Bueno.
¡DEE-ga-   BWEH-no.
meh!

Information.
Información.
een-for-ma-S'YOHN.

Long distance.
Larga distancia.
LAR-ga deess-TAHN-s'ya.

Please, the telephone number of _____.
Por favor, el número de teléfono de _____.
por fa-VOR, el NOO-meh-ro deh teh-LEH-fo-no deh _____.

That was a wrong number.
Fue un número equivocado.
fweh oon NOO-meh-ro eh-kee-vo-KA-doh.

Get me, please, number _____.
Comuníqueme, por favor, con el número _____.
ko-moo-NEE-keh-meh, por fa-VOR, kohn el NOO-meh-ro _____.

I want to call Los Angeles in the United States.
Quiero llamar Los Ángeles en los Estados Unidos.
KYEH-ro l'ya-MAR lohs AHN-heh-lehs en lohs ess-TA-dohs oo-NEE-dohs.

111

The number I am calling
  is _____ . . .
Estoy llamando el núm-
  ero _____ . . .
*ess-TOY l'ya-MAHN-doh el
  NOO-meh-ro _____ . . .*

extension . . .
extensión . . .
ex-ten-S'YOHN . . .

Must I wait long?
¿Debo esperar mucho tiempo?
¿DEH-bo ess-peh-RAR MOO-cho T'YEM-po?

How much is it per minute?
¿Cuánto cuesta por minuto?
¿KWAHN-toh KWESS-ta por mee-NOO-toh?

My number is 31-01-38.
Mi número es treinta y uno-cero uno-treinta y ocho.
*mee NOO-meh-ro ess TRAIN-ta ee OO-no SEH-ro OO-
no TRAIN-ta ee OH-cho.*

Mr. Duran, please.
El señor Durán, por favor.
el sen-YOR doo-RAHN, por fa-VOR.

What?
¿Cómo?
¿KO-mo?

He (she) isn't here.
No está aquí.
no ess-TA ah-KEE.

Hold the line!
¡No cuelgue!
¡no KWEL-geh!

**When is he (she) coming
  back?**
¿Cuándo vuelve?
¿KWAHN-do VWEL-veh?

Very well, I'll call back.
Bien, llamaré otra vez.
b'yen, l'ya-ma-REH OH-tra vess.

Can you take a message?
¡Puede tomar un recado?
¿PWEH-deh toh-MAR oon reh-KA-doh?

Ask him (her) to call me.
Digale que me llame.
DEE-ga-leh keh meh L'YA-meh.

I'll give you my number.
Le daré mi número.
leh da-REH mee NOO-meh-ro.

Who is speaking?
¿Quién habla?
¿k'yen AH-bla?

This is Mr. Smith speaking.
Habla el señor Smith.
Ah-bla el sen-YOR smith.

That is written: S–m–i–t--h.
Eso se escribe: S–m–i–t–h.
Eh-so seh es-KREE-beh: EH-seh EH-meh ee teh AH-cheh.

A	B	C	CH	D
ah	*beh*	*seh*	*cheh*	*deh*

E	F	G	H	I
eh	*EH-feh*	*heh*	*AH-cheh*	*ee*

J	K	L	LL	M
HO-ta	*ka*	*EH-leh*	*EHL-yeh*	*EH-meh*

N	Ñ	O	P	Q
EH-neh	*EHN-yeh*	*oh*	*peh*	*koo*

R	RR	S	T	U
EH-reh	*EH-rreh*	*EH-seh*	*teh*	*oo*

V	W	X
veh	*DOH-bleh veh*	*EH-kees*

Y	Z
ee-gree-YEH-ga	*SEH-ta*

A propósito: As American and English names are often strange to Spanish ears, you will find the spelled out alphabet very useful for spelling your name when you leave a message.

Where is the public telephone?
¿Dónde está el teléfono público?
¿DOHN-deh ess-TA el teh-LEH-fo-no POO-blee-ko?

The telephone book.
La guía telefónica.
la GHEE-ya teh-leh-FO-nee-ka.

Excuse me.	**What coin do I put in?**
Perdón.	¿Qué moneda debo echar?
pehr-DOHN.	*¿keh mo-NEH-da DEH-bo eh-CHAR?*

In Spain, tokens are used in public telephones.

A token, please.	**Another token.**
Una ficha, por favor.	Otra ficha.
OO-na FEE-cha, por fa-VOR.	*OH-tra FEE-cha.*

If there is no public telephone available:

May I use your phone?
¿Me permite usar su teléfono?
¿meh pehr-MEE-teh oo-SAR soo teh-LEH-fo-no?

It's a local call.
Es una llamada local.
ess OO-na l'ya-MA-da lo-CAHL.

Go ahead.	**The phone is over there.**
Siga no maś.	El teléfono esta allí.
SEE-ga no mahs.	*El teh-LEH-fo-no ess-TA ahl-YEE.*

How much do I owe you? **Nothing.**
¿Cuánto le debo?   Nada.
¿KWAHN-toh leh DEH-   *NA-da.*
  bo?

Thanks. You are very kind.
¡Gracias! Ud. es muy amable.
¡GRA-s'yahs! oo-STED ess mwee ah-MA-bleh.

18. Post Office and Telegrams

One of the first things one does when abroad is to write postcards—**tarjetas postales**—to friends and relatives. Here is how to mail them. You might also impress your friends by adding a few words in Spanish, which you will find at the end of this section.

Where is the post office?
¿Dónde está el correo?
¿DOHN-deh ess-TA el ko-RREH-oh?

Ten 50-centavo stamps.
Diez estampillas de a cincuenta.
dyess ess-tahm-PEEL-yahs deh ah seen-KWEHN-ta.

How much is needed?
¿Cuánto se necesita?
¿KWAHN-toh seh neh-seh-SEE-ta

Air mail.
Por avión.
por ahv-YOHN.

For a letter to the United States.
Para una carta a los Estados Unidos.
PA-ra OO-na KAR-ta ah los ess-TA-dohs oo-NEE-dohs.

. . . to Canada.
. . . al Canadá
. . . ahl ka-na-DA.

. . . to England.
. . . a Inglaterra.
. . . ah een-gla-TEH-ra.

. . . to Australia.
. . . a Australia.
. . . ah ow-STRAHL-ya.

For names of other important countries, see dictionary.

Registered.
Certificada.
sehr-tee-fee-KA-da.

Insured.
Asegurada.
ah-seh-goo-RA-da.

117

Where can I send a telegram?
¿Dónde puedo mandar un telegrama?
¿DOHN-deh PWEH-doh mahn-DAR oon teh-leh-GRA-ma?

How much is it per word?
¿Cuánto cuesta por palabra?
¿KWAHN-toh KWESS-ta por pa-LA-bra?

I need writing paper.
Necesito papel de escribir.
neh-seh-SEE-toh pa-PEL deh es-kree-BEER.

. . . envelopes.
. . . sobres.
. . . SO-brehs.

Can you lend me
¿Puede prestarme
¿PWEH-deh press-TAR-meh

. . . a pen?
. . . una pluma?
. . . OO-na PLOO-ma?

. . . a pencil?
. . . un lápiz?
. . . oon LA-peess?

. . . some stamps?
. . . algunas estampillas?
. . . ahl-GOO-nahs ess-tahm-PEEL-yahs?

Dear John,
Querido Juan,
keh-REE-doh hwan,

Dear Jane,
Querida Juanita,
keh-REE-da hwa-NEE-ta,

Best regards from Acapulco.
Recuerdos desde Acapulco.
reh-KWEHR-dohs DES-deh ah-ka-POOL-ko.

Best wishes to everyone.
Saludos a todos.
sal-LOO-dohs ah TOH-dohs.

I miss you.
Te estraño mucho.
teh ess-TRA-n'yo MOO-cho.

With fond regards,
Cariñosamente,
ka-reen-yo-sa-MEN-teh,

19. Seasons and the Weather

winter
el invierno
el een-V'YEHR-no

spring
la primavera
la pree-ma-VEH-ra

summer
el verano
el veh-RA-no

autumn
el otoño
el oh-TOHN-yo

How is the weather?
¿Qué tiempo hace?
¿keh T'YEM-po AH-seh?

The weather is fine.
Hace buen tiempo.
AH-seh bwehn T'YEM-po.

It's cold.
Hace frío.
AH-seh FREE-yo.

It's raining.
Está lloviendo.
ess-TA l'yo-V'YEN-doh.

I need an umbrella.
Necesito un paraguas.
neh-seh-SEE-toh oon pa-RA-gwahs.

. . . boots.
. . . botas.
. . . BO-tahs.

. . . a raincoat.
. . . un impermeable.
. . . oon eem-pehr-meh-AH-bleh.

It's snowing.
Está nevando.
ess-TA neh-VAHN-doh.

Do you like to ski?
¿Le gusta esquiar?
¿leh GOOS-ta ess-kee-YAR?

. . . to skate?
. . . patinar?
. . . pa-tee-NAR?

I want to rent skis.
Quiero alquilar esquíes.
K'YEH-ro ahl-kee-LAR ess-KEE-ess.

. . . skates
. . . patines.
. . . pa-TEE-nehs.

It's very hot today.
Hoy hace mucho calor.
oy AH-seh MOO-cho ka-LOR.

Let's go swimming.	**Where is the pool?**	**. . . the beach?**
Vamos a nadar.	¿Dónde está la piscina?	. . . la playa?
VA-mohs ah na-DAR.	*¿DOHN-deh ess-TA la pee-SEE-na?*	. . . *la PLA-ya?*

I want to rent a boat . . .
Quiero alquilar un bote . . .
K'YEH-no ahl-kee-LAR oon BO-teh . . .

. . . a mask and fins.
. . . una máscara y aletas.
. . . *OO-na MA-ska-ra ee ah-LEH-tahs.*

. . . air tanks.
. . . tanques de compresión.
. . . *TAHN-kehs deh kohm-preh-s'YOHN.*

Is it all right to swim here?
¿Está bien nadar aquí?
ess-TA b'yen na-DAR ah-KEE?

Are there sharks?
¿Hay tiburones?
I tee-boo-RO-nehs?

What is that big ship on the horizon?
¿Cuál es aquel vapor grande al horizonte?
¿keh es ah-KEL va-POR GRAHN-deh ahl oh-ree-SOHN-teh?

Is it a cargo ship?
¿Es un buque de carga?
¿ess oon BOO-keh deh KAR-ga?

No, it isn't.
No, no es.
no, no ess.

It's a passenger ship.
Es un vapor de pasajeros.
ess oon va-POR de pa-sa-HEH-rohs.

It travels to Venezuela, Colombia . . .
Viaja a Venezuela, Colombia . . .
V'YA-ha ah veh-nehz-WEH-la, ko-LOMB-ya . . .

Mexico and the Caribbean islands.
México y las islas del Caribe.
MEH-hee-ko ee lahs EE-slahs del ka-REE-beh.

Look at that beautiful yacht over there!
¡Mire aquel hermoso yate allá!
¡MEE-reh ah-KEL air-MO-so YA-teh ahl-L'YA!

I can't read the name . . .
No puedo leer el nombre . . .
no PWEH-doh leh-YAIR el NOHM-breh . . .

Wait, I can read it with my binoculars.
Espere, puedo leerlo con mis binoculares.
es-PEH-reh, PWEH-doh leh-YAIR-lo kohn mees bee-no-ku-LA-rehs.

It's called the "Siempre Feliz."*
Se llama el "Siempre Feliz."
seh l'YA-ma el "S'YEM-preh feh-LEESS."

---

* "Always Happy"

20. Sports and Festivals

The vocabulary for the following section is useful for those attending sporting and other events popular in Spanish countries. In addition, many Spanish-speaking cities celebrate historic and religious festivals from the Middle Ages and earlier. Be sure to find out when these take place in case you have a chance to witness one.

Do you like tennis?
¿Le gusta el tenis?
¿leh GOO-sta el TEN-nis?

Yes, indeed! I like it very much!
¡Claro! Me gusta mucho!
¡CLA-ro! meh GOO-sta MOO-cho!

There are tennis courts behind the hotel.
Hay canchas de ténis detrás del hotel.
Aye KAHN-chas deh TEN-nis deh-TRAHS del o-TEL.

We can reserve one.
Podemos reservar una.
po-DEH-mohs reh-zer-VAR OO-na.

But I don't have a racquet.
Pero no tengo raqueta.
PER-ro no TEN-go ra-KAY-ta.

Don't worry.
No se preocupe.
No seh preh-oh-KOO-peh.

We can rent one in the office.
Podrá alquilar una en la oficina.
po-DRA al-kee-LA OO-na en la oh-fee-SEE-na.

I would like to see a football game.
Me gustaría ver un partido de fútbol.
meh goo-sta-REE-ya vehr oon par-TEE-doh deh FOOT-bol.

123

There will be an important game next Sunday.
Habrá un partido importante el domingo.
ah-BRA oon par-TEE-doh eem-por-TAHN-teh el do-
MEEN-go.

Peru against Chile.
Perú contra Chile.
peh-ROO KOHN-tra CHEE-leh.

They say that Chile will win.
Se dice que Chile vencerá.
seh DEE-seh keh CHEE-leh ven-seh-RA.

Let's go! But I hope there won't be riots, like last year.
¡Vamos! Pero espero que no haya motines, como el año
pasado.
¡VA-mohs! PEH-ro ess-PEH-ro keh no AH-ya mo-TEE-
nehs, KO-mo el AHN-yo pa-SA-do.

Have you ever seen a bullfight?
¿Ha visto alguna vez una corrida de toros?
¿ah VEE-sto ahl-GOO-na vehz OO-na ko-RREE-doh deh
TOH-rohs?

Not yet. I would like to see one.
Todavía no. Me gustaría ver una.
toh-da-VEE-ya no. meh goo-sta-REE-ya vehr OO-na.

There will be one next Sunday.
Habrá una el domingo que viene.
ah-BRA OO-na el doh-MEEN-go keh V'YEH-neh.

A very well-known bullfighter is taking part.
Toma parte un torero muy conocido.
TOH-ma PAR-teh oon toh-REH-ro mwee ko-no-SEE-doh.

Don't you want to come with me?
¿No quiere venir conmigo?
¿No K'YEH-reh veh-NEER kohn-MEE-go?

With great pleasure, thanks.
Con mucho gusto, gracias.
kohn MOO-cho GOO-sto, GRA-s'yahs.

You will like it. It is very exciting . . .
Le gustará. Es muy emocionante . . .
leh goo-sta-RA. ess m'wee eh-mo-s'yo-NAHN-teh . . .

the music, the traditional costumes . . .
la musica, los trajes tradicionales . . .
la MOO-see-ka, lohs TRA-hehs tra-dee-s'yo-NA-lehs . . .

the public enthusiasm.
el entusiasmo del publico.
el en-too-S'YA-smo del POO-blee-ko.

It's a magnificent festive occasion for everyone.
Es una fiesta magnifica para todos.
ess OO-na F'YES-ta mahg-NEE-fee-ka PA-ra TOH-dohs.

Certainly. Except perhaps for the bull.
Claro. Excepto quizá para el toro.
KLA-ro. ex-SEP-toh kee-ZA PA-ra el TOH-ro.

21. Doctor and Dentist

Doctor

I feel ill.
Me siento enfermo.
meh S'YEN-toh en-FEHR-mo.

I need a doctor.
Necesito un médico.
neh-seh-SEE-toh oon MEH-dee-ko.

It's urgent.
Es urgente.
ess oor-HEN-teh.

When can he come?
¿Cuándo puede venir?
¿KWAHN-do PWEH-deh veh-NEER?

Well, what's wrong with you?
Bueno, ¿qué le pasa?
BWEH-no, ¿keh leh PA-sa?

I don't feel well.
No me siento bien.
no meh S'YEN-toh b'yen.

Where does it hurt?
¿Dónde le duele?
¿DOHN-deh leh DWEH-leh?

Here.
Aquí.
ah-KEE.

I have a pain ......
Tengo dolor ...
TEN-go doh-LOR ...

in my head.
... de cabeza.
... deh ka-BEH-sa.

He (she) has a pain ...
Tiene dolor ...
T'YEH-neh doh-LOR ...

... in the throat.
... de garganta.
... deh gar-GAHN-ta.

... in the ear.
... de oído.
... deh oh-EE-doh.

. . . in the stomach.
.. de estómago.
. . . *deh ess-TOH-ma-go.*

. . . in the back.
. . . de espalda.
. . . *deh ess-PAHL-da.*

I hurt my leg.
Me hice daño en la pierna.
meh EE-seh DAHN-yo en
  la P'YEHR-na.

. . . my ankle.
. . . el tobillo.
. . . *el toh-BEEL-yo.*

. . . my foot.
. . . el pie.
. . . *el p'yeh.*

. . . my arm.
. . . el brazo.
. . . *el BRA-so.*

. . . my hand.
. . . la mano.
. . . *la MA-no.*

I am dizzy
Estoy mareado.
ess-TOY ma-reh-AH-doh.

I have a fever.
Tengo fiebre.
TEN-go F'YEH-breh.

I can't sleep.
No puedo dormir.
no PWEH-doh dor-MEER.

I have diarrhea.
Tengo diarrea.
TEN-go d'ya-RREH-ah.

A propósito: The centigrade scale is also used to measure body temperature. The normal body temperature is 36.7 degrees (98 degrees Fahrenheit). So if you have anything higher than that, you have a temperature—**Ud. tiene calentura**.

Since when?
¿Desde cuándo?
¿DES-deh KWAHN-doh?

Since yesterday.
Desde ayer.
Des-deh ah-YEHR.

Since two days ago.
Desde hace dos días.
DES-deh AH-seh dohs DEE-yahs.

What have you eaten?
¿Qué ha comido?
¿keh ah ko-MEE-doh?

Undress.
Desvístase.
des-VEESS-ta-seh.

Lie down.
Acuéstese.
ah-KWESS-teh-
      seh.

Stand up.
Levántase.
leh-VAHN-ta-seh.

Breathe deeply.
Respire hondo.
res-PEE-reh OHN-doh.

Open your mouth.
Abra la boca.
AH-bra la BO-ka.

Show me your tongue.
Enséñeme la lengua.
en-SEN-yeh-meh la LEN-gwah.

Cough.
Tosa.
TOH-sa.

Get dressed.
Vístase.
VEESS-ta-seh.

You must . . .	**. . . stay in bed.**	**. . . go to the hospital.**
Tiene que . . .	. . . quedarse en cama.	. . . ir al hospital.
TYEH-neh keh . . .	*. . . key-DAR-seh en KA-ma.*	*. . . eer ahl ohs-pee-TAHL.*

Take this prescription.
Tome esta receta.
TOH-meh ESS-ta reh-SEH-ta.

Take these pills.
Tome estas pastillas.
TOH-meh ESS-tahs pahs-TEEL-yahs.

Is it serious?
¿Es serio?
¿ess SEH-r'yo?

It's not serious.
No es serio.
No ess SEH-r'yo.

Don't worry.
No se preocupe.
no seh preh-oh-KOO-peh.

You have . . .	**. . . indigestion.**	**. . . an infection.**
Tiene . . .	. . . indigestión.	. . . una infeccíon.
T'YEH-neh . . .	*. . . een-dee-hehs-T'YOHN.*	*. . . OO-na een-fek-S'YOHN.*

. . . a cold.
. . . un resfriado.
. . . oon res-free-AH-doh.

. . . liver trouble.
. . . un problema del hígado.
. . . oon pro-BLEH-ma del EE-ga-doh.

. . . appendicitis.
. . . apendicitis.
. . . ah-pen-dee-SEE-teess.

. . . a heart attack.
. . . un ataque cardíaco.
. . . oon ah-TA-keh car-DEE-ah-ko.

Be careful.
Tenga cuidado.
TEN-ga kwee-DA-doh.

Don't eat too much.
No coma demasiado.
no KO-ma deh-ma-S'YA-doh.

Don't drink any alcohol.
No tome nada de alcohol.
no TOH-meh NA-da deh ahl-ko-OHL.

How do you feel today?
¿Qué tal se siente hoy?
¿keh tahl seh S'YEN-teh oy?

Badly.
Mal.
mahl.

Better.
Mejor.
meh-HOR.

Much better.
Mucho mejor.
MOO-cho meh-HOR.

Dentist

In the unlikely event that the dentist should hurt you, tell him ¡Pare! "Stop!" or ¡Espere un momento! "Wait a moment!" until you have time to regain your courage.

Can you recommend a dentist?
¿Puede recomendar un dentista?
¿PWEH-deh reh-ko-men-DAR oon den-TEES-ta?

I have a toothache.
Tengo un dolor de muela.
TEN-go oon doh-LOR deh MWEH-la.

It hurts here.
Me duele aquí.
meh DWEH-leh ah-KEE.

There is an infection.
Hay una infección.
I OO-na een-fek-S'YOHN.

You need a filling.
Necesita una calza.
neh-seh-SEE-ta OO-na KAHL-sa.

Will it take long?
¿Se demorará mucho?
¿seh deh-mo-ra-RA MOO-cho?

Just fix it temporarily.
Arréglela provisionalmente.
ah-RREH-gleh-la pro-vee-s'yo-nahl-MEN-teh.

This tooth must come out.
Tiene que sacarse esta muela.
T'YEH-neh keh sa-KAR-seh ESS-ta MWEH-la.

An injection for pain, please.
Una inyección para el dolor, por favor.
OO-na een-yek-S'YOHN PA-ra el doh-LOR, por fa-VOR.

Does it hurt?
¿Le duele?
¿leh DWEH-leh

A little.
Un poco.
oon PO-ko.

Not at all.
En absoluto.
en ahb-so-LOO-toh.

Is that all?
¿Eso es todo?
¿EH-so ess TOH-doh?

What do I owe you?
¿Cuánto le debo?
¿KWAHN-toh leh DEH-bo?

22. Problems and Police

Although the situations suggested below may never happen to you, the words are useful to know, just in case!

Go away!
¡Váyase!
¡VA-ya-seh!

Leave me alone!
¡Déjeme tranquila!
¡DEH-heh-meh trahn-KEE-la!

Or I'll call a policeman.
O llamo a un policía.
oh L'YA-mo ah oon po-lee-SEE-ya.

Help!
¡Socorro!
¡so-KO-rro!

Police!
¡Policía!
¡po-lee-SEE-ya!

What's going on?
¿Qué es lo que pasa?
¿keh ess lo keh PA-sa?

This man is annoying me.
Este hombre me está molestando.
ESS-teh OHM-breh meh ess-TA mo-les-TAHN-doh.

Where is the police station?
¿Dónde está el cuartel de policía?
¿DOHN-deh ess-TA el kwahr-TEL deh po-lee-SEE-ya?

I've lost . . .
He perdido . . .
eh perh-dee-doh . . .

. . . my wallet.
. . . la cartera.
. . . la kar-TEH-ra.

. . . my suitcase.
. . . la maleta.
. . . la ma-LEH-ta.

. . . my passport.
. . . el pasaporte.
. . . el pa-sa-POR-teh.

. . . my watch.
. . . el reloj.
. . . el reh-LO.

. . . jewelry.
. . . las prendas.
. . . lahs PREN-dahs.

. . . my traveler's checks.
. . . los cheques de viajero.
. . . lohs chek-kehs deh v'ya-HEH-ro.

Stop that man!
¡Paren a ese hombre!
¡PA-ren ah EH-seh OHM-breh!

That's the one!
¡Ese es!
¡EH-seh ess!

He robbed me.
Me robó.
meh ro-BO.

I wish to make a complaint.
Quiero presentar una queja.
KYEH-ro preh-sen-TAR OO-na KEH-ha.

Calm down!
¡Cálmese!
¡KAHL-meh-seh!

Don't worry!
¡No se preocupe!
¡no seh preh-oh-KOO-peh!

Remain here!
¡Quédese aquí!
¡KEH-deh-seh ah-KEE!

Is this your property?
¿Es ésta su propiedad?
¡ess ESS-ta soo pro-pee-eh-DAHD?

Fill in this form.
Llene este formulario.
L'YEH-neh ESS-teh for-moo-LAR-yo.

This man says that . . .
Este hombre dice que . . .
ESS-teh OHM-breh DEE-seh keh . . .

. . . it's a misunderstanding.
. . . es un malentendido
. . . ess oon mahl-en-ten-DEE-doh.

Here are your things.
Aquí tiene sus cosas.
ah-KEE T'YEH-neh sooss KO-sahs.

Thank you!
¡Gracias!
¡GRA-s'yahs!

Can I go now?
¿Puedo irme ahora?
¿PWEH-doh EER-meh ah-OH-ra?

Wait!
¡Espere!
¡ess-PEH-reh!

The passport is missing.
Falta el pasaporte.
FAHL-ta el pa-sa-POR-teh.

I want to notify the consulate.
Quiero notificar el consulado.
K'YEH-ro no-tee-fee-KAR el kohn-soo-LA-doh.

A propósito: Despite the subject matter at the beginning of this section, ladies should not be alarmed if appreciative comments are made to them by men who stroll by, *if* the commentators continue to stroll in the opposite direction. It is simply an old Spanish custom called **el piropo** and merely expresses one's admiration of the girl or woman one has just passed.

23. Housekeeping

The following chapter will be especially interesting for those who plan to stay longer in a Spanish country or have occasion to employ Spanish-speaking baby sitters or household help, abroad or even at home.

What is your name?
¿Cómo se llama Ud.?
¿KO-mo seh L'YA-ma oo-STED?

Where have you worked before?
¿Dónde ha trabajado antes?
¿DOHN-deh ah tra-ba-HA-doh AHN-tehs?

Do you know how to cook?
¿Sabe cocinar?
¿SA-beh ko-see-NAR?

Do you know how to take care of a baby?
¿Sabe cuidar un bebé?
¿SA-beh kwee-DAR oon beh-BEH?

This is your room.
Ésta es su habitación.
ESS-ta ess soo ah-bee-ta-S'YOHN.

Thursday will be your day off.
El jueves será su día libre.
el HWEH-vehs seh-RA soo DEE-ya LEE-breh.

We will pay you ____ every week.
Le pagaremos ____ cada semana.
leh pa-ga-REH-mohs ____ KA-da seh-MA-na.

Please clean . . .   **. . . the living room.**
Por favor, limpie . . .   . . . la sala.
por fa-VOR, LEEM-   *. . . la SA-la.*
p'yeh . . .

. . . the dining room.
. . . el comedor.
. . . el ko-meh-DOR.

. . . the bedroom.
. . . el dormitorio.
. . . el dor-mee-TOR-yo.

. . . the bathroom.
. . . el cuarto de baño.
. . . el KWAHR-toh deh
   BAHN-yo.

. . . the kitchen.
. . . la cocina.
. . . la ko-SEE-na.

Wash the dishes.
Lave los platos.
LA-veh los PLA-tohs.

Sweep the floor.
Barra el piso.
BA-rra el PEE-so.

Use the vacuum cleaner.
Use la aspiradora.
OO-seh la ahs-pee-ra-
   DOH-ra.

. . . the broom.
. . . la escoba.
. . . la ess-KO-ba.

Polish the silver.
Limpie los cubiertos de plata.
LEEM-p'yeh los koob-YEHR-tohs deh PLA-ta.

Make the beds.
Tienda las camas.
T'YEN-da las KA-mahs.

Change the sheets.
Cambie las sábanas.
KAHM-b'yeh las SA-ba-
   nahs.

Wash this.
Lave esto.
LA-veh ESS-toh.

Iron this.
Planche esto.
PLAHN-cheh ESS-toh.

Go to the market.
Vaya al mercado.
VA-ya ahl mehr-KA-doh.

Have you finished?
¿Ha terminado?
¿ah tehr-mee-NA-doh?

What do we need?
¿Qué necesitamos?
¿keh neh-seh-see-TA-mohs?

Here is the list.
Aquí está la lista.
ah-KEE ess-TA la
   LEESTA.

Put the meat in the refrigerator.
Ponga la carne en la nevera.
POHN-ga la KAR-neh en la neh-VEH-ra.

If someone calls,
Si alguien llama,
see AHL-g'yen L'YA-ma,

write the name here.
escriba el nombre aquí.
ess-KREE-ba el NOHM-breh ah-KEE.

I'll be at this number.
Estaré en este número.
ess-ta-REH en ESS-teh NOO-meh-ro.

I'll be back at 4 o'clock.
Regresaré a las cuatro.
reh-greh-sa-REH ah las KWA-tro.

Feed the baby at _____.
Dele a comer al bebé a las _____.
DEH-leh ah ko-MEHR ahl beh-BEH ah lahs _____.

Bathe the child.
Bañe al niño.
BAHN-yeh ahl NEEN-yo.

Put him to bed at _____.
Acuéstelo a las _____.
ah-KWESS-teh-lo ah lahs _____.

Did anyone call?
¿Ha llamado alguien?
¿ah l'ya-MA-doh AHL-g'yen?

We are having guests for dinner.
Tenemos invitados para la cena.
teh-NEH-mohs een-vee-TA-dohs PA-ra la SEH-na.

Set the table for eight people.
Ponga la mesa para ocho personas.
POHN-ga la MEH-sa PA-ra OH-cho, pehr-SO-nahs.

Serve dinner at 9 o'clock.
Sirva la cena a las nueve.
SEER-va la SEH-na ah lahs NWEH-veh.

Put these flowers on the table.
Ponga estas flores en la mesa.
POHN-ga ESS-tahs FLO-rehs en la MEH-sa.

There's someone at the door.
Hay alguien en la puerta.
I AHL-g'yen en la PWEHR-ta.

Open the door please.
Abra la puerta, por favor.
AH-bra la PWEHR-ta, por fa-VOR.

24. Some Business Phrases

You will find the short phrases and vocabulary in this section extremely useful if you are on a business trip to Latin America or to Spain. While it is true that English is the most prominent foreign language used in the Spanish-speaking world and that efficient interpreters are available, these phrases will add another dimension to your contacts with your Spanish and Latin American business associates. The fact that you have made the effort to master some business expressions will be a compliment to your hosts and will indicate that you, by using some phrases in their language, are reciprocating their traditional politeness.

Good morning. Is Mr. Gómez in?
Buenos días. ¿Está el Sr. Gómez?
BWEH-nohs DEE-yas. ess-TA el sen-YOR GO-mehs?

I have an appointment with him.
Tengo cita con él.
TEN-go SEE-ta kohn el.

My name is _____ _____.
Me llamo _____ _____.
meh L'YA-mo _____ _____.

Here is my card.
Aquí está mi tarjeta.
ah-KEE ess-TA mee tar-HEH-ta.

He is expecting you.
El lo espera.
el lo ess-PEH-ra.

This way please.
Por aquí, por favor.
por ah-KEE, por fa-VOR.

Welcome to Argentina, Mr. Bell.
Bienvenido a Argentina, Señor Bell.
b'yen-veh-NEE-doh ah ar-hehn-TEE-na, sen-YOR Bell.

141

Do you like Buenos Aires?
Le gusta Buenos Aires?
leh GOO-sta BWEH-nohs I-rehs?

Very much! It's a very beautiful city.
¡Muchísimo! Es una ciudad muy bella.
*¡moo-CHEE-see-mo! Ess OO-na s'yoo-DAHD mwee
BEH-l'ya.*

Thank you for this appointment.
Le agradezco esta cita.
leh ah-gra-DESS-ko ESS-ta SEE-ta.

We understand that you are interested . . .
Entendemos que Ud. está interesado . . .
*en-ten-DEH-mohs keh oo-STED ess-TA een-teh-reh-SA-
doh . . .*

. . . in our business machines.
. . . en nuestras máquinas de negocios.
. . . en NWESS-trahs MA-kee-nahs deh neh-GO-s'yohs.

This is our latest catalog.
Aquí tiene nuestro último catálogo.
*ah-KEE T'YEH-neh NWESS-troh OOL-tee-mo ka-TA-lo-
go.*

These are our new models . . .
Estos son nuestros nuevos modelos . . .
*ESS-tohs sohn NWEHS-trohs NWEH-vohs mo-DEH-
lohs . . .*

. . . of computers and copiers.
. . . de computadoras y de copiadoras.
*. . . deh kohm-poo-ta-DOH-rahs ee deh ko-p'ya-DOH-
rahs.*

Thank you. It looks interesting.
Gracias. Parece interesante.
GRAH-s'yahs. pa-REH-seh een-teh-reh-SAHN-teh.

Can you come back Wednesday morning?
¿Puede volver el miercoles por la mañana?
*¿PWEH-deh vol-VEHR el M'YEHR-ko-lehs por la mahn-
YA-na?*

We wish to place an order.
Deseamos hacer un pedido.
deh-seh-AH-mohs ah-SEHR oon peh-DEE-doh.

We expect a discount of _____ %.
Esperamos un descuento del _____ por ciento.
*ess-peh-RA-mohs oon dess-KWEN-toh del _____ por
S'YEHN-toh.*

What are the terms of payment?
¿Cuáles son los términos de pago?
¿KWA-lehs sohn lohs TEHR-mee-nohs deh PA-go?

By Bank Draft 30-day—60-day—90-day.
Por giro bancario de 30 días—60 días—90 días.
*por HEE-ro bahn-KA-ryo deh TRAIN-ta DEE-yahs—seh-
SEN-ta DEE-yahs—no-VEN-ta DEE-yahs.*

Irrevocable letter of credit.
Carta de crédito irrevocable.
KAR-ta deh KREH-dee-toh eer-reh-vo-KA-bleh.

(N.B.: FOB CIF are understood internationally.)

We have an account with the _____ Bank.
Tenemos cuenta con el Banco _____.
teh-NEH-mohs KWEN-ta kohn el BAHN-ko _____.

When can we expect shipment? . . . delivery?
¿Cuándo podemos esperar el envío . . . la entrega?
*¿KWAHN-doh po-DEH-mohs ess-peh-RAR el en-VEE-yo
. . . la en-TREH-ga?*

Are these your best terms?
¿Son éstos sus mejores términos?
¿sohn ESS-tohs soos me-HO-rehs TEHR-mee-nohs?

Would you like to sign a contract?
¿Le gustaría firmar un contrato?
¿leh goo-sta-REE-ya feer-MAR oon kohn-TRA-toh?

We are in agreement, aren't we?
Estamos de acuerdo, ¿no?
ess-TA-mohs deh ah-KWEHR-doh, no?

We need time to examine the contract.
Necesitamos tiempo para examinar el contrato.
*neh-seh-see-TA-mohs t'YEM-po PA-ra ek-sa-mee-NAR el
   kohn-TRA-toh.*

Our lawyers will contact you.
Nuestros abogados le avisarán.
NWEH-strohs ah-bo-GA-dohs leh ah-vee-sa-RAHN.

It's a pleasure to do business with you.
Es un placer tratar de negocios con Ud.
*ess oon pla-SEHR tra-TAR deh neh-GO-s'yohs kohn oo-
   STED.*

We would like to invite you to dinner.
Nos gustaría invitarle a comer.
nohs goo-sta-REE-ya een-vee-TAR-leh ah-ko-MEHR.

We will call for you at the hotel at 8.
Le buscaremos al hotel a las ocho.
leh boo-ska-REH-mohs ahl o-tel a lahs O-cho.

I thank you . . . for the invitation.
Muchas gracias . . . por la invitación.
MOO-chahs GRA-s'yahs . . . por la een-vee-ta-s'YOHN.

. . . for the dinner.   **. . . for everything.**
. . . por la comida.   . . . por todo.
. . . por la ko-MEE-da.   *. . . por TOH-doh.*

It was a great pleasure to meet you.
Fue un gran placer conocerlo.
fweh oon grahn pla-SEHR ko-no-SEHR-lo.

Whenever you visit America
Cuando visite América
KWAHN-doh vee-SEE-teh ah-MEH-ree-ka

. . . please tell us in advance.
. . . sírvase informarnos de antemano.
. . . SEER-va-seh een-FOR-mar-nohs deh AHN-teh-ma-no.

25. Una Buena Noticia: Spanish Words You Already Know

English and Spanish share a great number of words. This comes from the influence of Latin, the language of the Roman Empire which once ruled Western and Southern Europe and England. In modern Spanish these words are easy to recognize when one makes a slight spelling change, usually in the last syllable. They then become easy to understand and say, especially since you are already familiar with the Spanish pronunciation as presented throughout this book.

Here are some of these words according to their spelling changes.

English words ending in **-tion** are equivalent to Spanish words ending in **-ción**. Here are just a few:

condición	exposición
inmigración	revolución
identificación	interpretación
imitación	nación
emoción	hesitación

and hundreds of others.

English words ending in **ion** can become Spanish simply by adding an accent to the final "o."

unión	fusión
confusión	explosión
conclusión	invasión

Words ending in a final **al** or **ar** are often the same in Spanish and English:

fatal	general
animal	principal
liberal	popular
final	particular
sentimental	

Words ending in **ism** add an "o" in Spanish, as do words ending in **ment**:

optimismo	capitalismo
pesimismo	documento
socialismo	suplimento

Remember that Spanish avoids double letters—except for "rr" and "ll" (both of which are considered letters in their own right) and occasionally a double "c" (cc).

The final **ous** changes to **oso** in Spanish:

  vigoroso, fabuloso, generoso, ridiculoso

Many English words ending in **-it, -ite, -ito, -ate** or **-ic** end in **o** in Spanish.

depósito	débito
favorito	artístico
depósito	fantástico
crédito	plástico
mérito	modesto

English words ending in **-ent** or **-ant** add an **-e** in Spanish:

permanente	**importante**
presidente	**residente**
ingrediente	**inmigrante**
	(the first "m" changes to an "n"),

inteligente (note the single "l").

For English words ending in **-ive** change the "e" to "o":

  positivo, motivo, executivo, expansivo

The English suffix **-ble** does not change:

posible, imposible, probable, responsable.

The English suffix **-ty** frequently changes to **-dad**.

realidad, posibilidad, sinceridad, utilidad, agilidad facilidad and also, with **-tad** instead of **-dad** libertad.

Many English words ending in **-ary** translate into Spanish through using the ending **-ario**:

necesario	reaccionario
ordinario	sanitario
temporario	diccionario
extraordinario	

26. A New Type of Dictionary

The following dictionary supplies a list of English words and their translation into Spanish, which will enable you to make up your own sentences in addition to those given in the phrase book. By using these words, in conjunction with the following advice and short cuts, you will be able to make up hundreds of sentences by yourself. In general, only one Spanish equivalent is given for each English word—the one most useful to you—so you won't be in doubt about which word to use. Every word in this dictionary is followed by the phonetic pronunciation, so you will have no difficulty being understood.

All nouns are either masculine or feminine. If a noun ends in **-o** it is usually masculine; if it ends in **-a** it is usually feminine. Any *exceptions* are noted by "(m)" or "(f)" after the noun in the dictionary.

Adjectives usually follow the noun they go with. All adjectives in this dictionary are given in the masculine form only. If the adjective ends in **-o**, you must change the ending to **-a** when it goes with a feminine noun:

> the white hat   **el sombrero blanco**
> (**El** is the masculine word for "the.")
> the white house   **la casa blanca**
> (**La** is the feminine word for "the.")

If the adjective does not end in **-o**, it is generally the same for both masculine and feminine.

Plurals are formed by adding **-s** to words ending in a vowel, or **-es** to words ending in a consonant. If a noun is plural, the article and adjectives that go with it must be in the plural form too:

> the white hats   **los sombreros blancos**
> (**Los** is the masculine plural word for "the.")
> the white houses   **las casas blancas**
> (**Las** is the feminine plural word for "the.")

The verbs in the dictionary are given in the infinitive form. In actual use, their endings change according to the subject. Although a full grammatical explanation is not within the scope of this book, the following explanations will help you to use and recognize the present tense of most of the verbs in the dictonary.

Verbs are divided into three groups, or "conjugations," according to their infinitive endings: **-ar, -er, and -ir.** **Hablar** (to speak), **aprender** (to learn), and **vivir** (to live) are examples of the first, second, and third conjugations. There are five important forms for each tense, depending on the "person" referred to. You can carry on a great deal of conversation using the present tense. Here is the present of **hablar,** which can serve as a model for all verbs of the first group:

(yo) hablo	I speak *or* I am speaking
(tú) hablas	you speak *or* you (familiar) are speaking
(él, ella usted) habla	he, she speaks, you (sg) speak *or* he, she is speaking, you are speaking
(nosotros, nosotras) hablamos	we (m and f) speak *or* we are speaking
(ellos, ellas, ustedes) hablan	they (m and f), you (pl) speak *or* they, you are speaking

Following the same order, the present tense forms for **aprender** and **vivir,** our examples of the second and third verb conjugations, are:

aprendo, aprendes, aprende, aprendemos, aprenden
vivo, vives, vive, vivimos, viven

Did you notice that these last two groups are almost the same?

In conversation the words for "I," "you," "he," "she," etc. are frequently dropped, because the ending of the verb shows the person referred to. We put these pronouns in parentheses to remind you of this. By listening to the endings **-o, -s, -a** *or* **-e, mos,** and **-n,** you can tell which person is doing the action. We have not indicated a pronoun for "it" as in Spanish everything is masculine or feminine and therefore "it" is "he" or "she." **Usted (UD.)** and **tú** both mean "you." However, you should ordinarily use **Ud.,** the polite form. **Tú** is the familiar form, used within the family, between close friends, among students, and to children.

Although the Spanish present tense of verbs is equivalent to both the English simple present tense and the present progressive tense, you can also use the Spanish present participle, with the present tense form of **estar** (to be), exactly like the English progressive. The present participle ends in **-ando** for the first conjugation and **-iendo,** for the second and third conjugations:

> I am eating.   **Yo estoy comiendo.**
> She is speaking.   **Ella está hablando.**

As some of the most important verbs are irregular, we have included such forms in sections of the phrase book at the time and place you will need to use them. To help you form your own sentences, the present tense of "to be," "to have," "to go," "to come," and "to want" is given in the dictionary as well.

As we have pointed out, you can do a lot of communicating by using simply the present tense. But, in addition, you can use the infinitive to express a variety of other concepts. To say something must be done or is necessary, use **es necesario** directly with the infinitive:

> I must leave.   **Es necesario partir.**

To say you want to do something or to invite someone to do something, use **querer** (to want) with the infinitive of the second verb:

> I want to go.   **Quiero ir.**
> Do you want to go?   **¿Quiere ir?**

For the negative, use **no**:

> I don't want to go.   **No quiero ir.**

An easy way to express what will happen in the future is to use a present form of **ir** (to go)—**voy, vas, va, vamos, van**—with a (to) followed by the infinitive:

> I am going to speak.   **Voy a hablar.**

The easiest way to give commands or make requests is to put **sírvase** in front of the infinitive:

> Come in!   **¡Sírvase entrar!**
> Don't come in!   **¡Sírvase no entrar!**

To form the perfect tense (i.e., "I have spoken," etc.) use the present tense of the verb **haber,** which is **he, has, ha, hemos, han,** combined with the past participle of the verb you want to use. The **-ar** verbs change their ending to **-ado** for the past participle (**hablar—hablado**) while the **-er** and **-ir** verbs generally change to **-ido** (**aprender—aprendido**).

> I have spoken *or* I spoke   **He hablado**

For basic conversational purposes the perfect tense can double in use for the past tense.

When you see a verb with **-se** attached to the infinitive in the dictionary it means that it is reflexive and must use the reflexive pronouns, **me, te, se,** and **nos** with the verb:

> to get up   **levantarse**
> I get up.   **(Yo) me levanto.**

Object pronouns are given within the dictionary. They come before the verb, except that when used with infinitives and imperatives they follow and are attached:

> I see her.   **(Yo) la veo.**
> I don't want to see her.   **No quiero verla.**

The possessive of nouns is expressed by **de**:

Robert's house   **la casa de Roberto**

Possessive pronouns are listed in the dictionary. Observe that these pronouns agree in gender and number with the noun to which they refer (not with the gender of the person possessing as in English):

That hat is his (hers).   **Este sombrero es el suyo.**
This house is his (hers).   **Esta casa es la suya.**

With this advice and the indications given within the dictionary itself, you will be able to use this communicating dictionary for making up countless sentences on your own and to converse with anyone you may meet.

There is, of course, much more to Spanish than these few suggestions we have given you—including the subtleties and irregularities of the Spanish verbs, diminutives, augmentatives, the special use of pronouns, and the numerous idioms and sayings that reflect the wisdom, poetry, and history of Spanish culture. But you can effectively use this selected basic vocabulary as an important step, or even a springboard, to enter the wonderful world that is the Spanish heritage and, by practice, absorb and constantly improve your command of this beautiful language.

For, as the Spanish say, **El apetito viene comiendo**—"Appetite comes with eating." Once you see how easy this book makes communicating in Spanish and how rewarding it is to speak to people in their own language, you will have the impetus to progress on your own.

A

a, an	un (m), una (f)	*oon, OO-na*
(to be) able	poder	*po-DEHR*
about (concerning)	acerca de	*ah-SEHR-ka deh*
above	sobre	*SO-breh*
absent	ausente	*ow-SEN-teh*
accept	aceptar	*ah-sep-TAR*
accident	accidente (m)	*ahk-see-DEN-teh*
account	cuenta	*KWEN-ta*
across	a través de	*ah tra-VEHS deh*
act	acto	*AHK-toh*
actor	actor	*ahk-TOR*
actress	actriz	*ahk-TREESS*
address	dirección (f)	*dee-rek-S'YOHN*
admission	admisión (f)	*ahd-mee-S'YOHN*
advertisement	anuncio	*ah-NOON-s'yo*
advice	consejo	*kohn-SEH-ho*
(to be) afraid	tener miedo	*teh-NEHR M'YEH-doh*
Africa	África	*AH-free-ka*
after	después	*dess-PWEHSS*
afternoon	tarde (f)	*TAR-deh*
again	de nuevo	*deh NWEH-vo*
against	contra	*KOHN-tra*
age	edad (f)	*eh-DAHD*
agency	agencia	*ah-HEN-s'ya*

agent	agente (m)	*ah-HEN-teh*
ago	hace	*AH-seh*
(See page 24 for an example.)		
(to) agree	concordar	*kohn-kor-DAR*
ahead	adelante	*ah-deh-LAHN-teh*
air	aire (m)	*I-reh*
air-conditioned	aire acondicionado	*I-reh ah-kohn-dee-s'yo-NA-doh*
air mail	correo aéreo	*ko-RREH-oh ah-EH-reh-oh*
airplane	avión (m)	*ahv-YOHN*
airport	aeropuerto	*ah-eh-ro-PWER-toh*
all	todo	*TOH-doh*
That's all!	¡Eso es todo!	*¡ES-so ess TOH-doh!*
(to) allow	permitir	*pehr-mee-TEER*
all right	está bien	*ess-TA b'yen*
almost	casi	*KA-see*
alone	solo	*SO-lo*
already	ya	*ya*
also	también	*tahm-B'YEN*
always	siempre	*SYEM-preh*
(I) am (permanent status)	soy	*soy*
(I) am (location or temporary status)	estoy	*ess-TOY*

America	América	*ah-MEH-ree-kA*
American	americano	*ah-meh-ree-KA-no*
amusing	divertido	*dee-ver-TEE-doh*
and	y	*ee*
angry	enojado	*eh-no-HA-doh*
animal	animal (m)	*ah-nee-MAHL*
ankle	tobillo	*toh-BEEL-yo*
annoying	molesto	*mo-LESS-toh*
another	otro	*OH-tro*
answer	respuesta	*ress-PWESS-ta*
antiseptic	antiséptico	*ahn-tee-SEP-tee-ko*
any	cualquier	*kwahl-K'YEHR*
anyone	alguien	*AHL-g'yen*
anyone (at all)	cualquiera	*kwahl-K'YEH-ra*
anything	algo	*AHL-go*
anywhere	en cualquier parte	*en kwahl-K'YEHR PAR-teh*
apartment	apartamento	*ah-par-ta-MEN-toh*
apple	manzana	*mahn-SA-na*
appointment	cita	*SEE-ta*
April	abril	*ah-BREEL*
Arab	árabe (m or f)	*AH-ra-beh*
Arabic (language)	árabe	*AH-ra-beh*
architecture	arquitectura	*ar-kee-tek-TOO-ra*
are (permanent status)		
(**you** sg.) **are**	(Ud.) es	*ess*
(**we**) **are**	(nosotros) somos	*SO-mohs*
(**they, you** pl.) **are**	(ellos, ellas, Uds.) son	*sohn*

are (location or temporary status)

(you sg.**) are**	(Ud.) está	*ess-TA*
(we) are	(nosotros) estamos	*ess-TA-mohs*
(they, you pl.**) are**	(ellos, ellas, Uds.) están	*ess-TAHN*
(there) are	hay	*I*
Argentina	Argentina	*ar-hen-TEE-na*
Argentinian	Argentino	*ar-hen-TEE-no*
arm	brazo	*BRA-so*
army	ejército	*eh-HEHR-see-toh*
around (surrounding)	alrededor	*ahl-reh-deh-DOR*
around (approximately)	alrededor de	*ahl-reh-deh-DOR deh*
(to) arrive	llegar	*l'yeh-GAR*
art	arte (m)	*AR-teh*
artist (m or f)	artista	*ar-TEESS-ta*
as	como	*KO-mo*
Asia	Asia	*AH-s'ya*
(to) ask (a question)	preguntar	*preh-goon-TAR*
(to) ask for	pedir	*peh-DEER*
asleep	dormido	*dor-MEE-doh*
asparagus	espárrago	*ess-PA-rra-go*
aspirin	aspirina	*ahs-pee-REE-na*

ass	asno	*AHS-no*
assortment	surtido	*soor-TEE-doh*
at (location)	en	*en*
at (time)	a	*ah*
Atlantic	Atlántico	*aht-LAHN-tee-ko*
atomic	atómico	*ah-TOH-mee-ko*
August	agosto	*ah-GOHS-toh*
aunt	tía	*TEE-ya*
Australia	Australia	*ows-TRA-l'ya*
Australian	australiano	*ows-tra-L'YA-no*
Austria	Austria	*OWS-tree-ya*
author	autor (m)	*ow-TOR*
automatic	automático	*ow-toh-MA-tee-ko*
automobile	automóvil	*ow-toh-MO-veel*
autumn	otoño	*oh-TOHN-yo*
(to) avoid	evitar	*eh-vee-TAR*

B

baby	bebé (m)	*beh-BEH*
bachelor	soltero	*sohl-TEH-ro*
back (part of body)	espalda	*ess-PAHL-da*
bacon	tocino	*toh-SEE-no*
bad	malo	*MA-lo*
baggage	equipaje (m)	*eh-kee-PA-heh*
banana	plátano	*PLA-ta-no*
bandage	venda	*VEN-da*

bank	banco	*BAHN-ko*
bar	bar (m)	*bar*
barber	barbero	*bar-BEH-ro*
basement	sótano	*SO-ta-no*
bath	baño	*BAHN-yo*
bathing suit	traje de baño (m)	*TRA-heh deh BAHN-yo*
bathroom	cuarto de baño	*KWAHR-toh deh BAHN-yo*
battery	batería	*ba-teh-REE-ya*
battle	batalla	*ba-TAHL-ya*
(to) be (perma- nent status)	ser	*sehr*

(See also "am," "is," "are," "was," "were," "been.")

| (to) be (location or temporary status) | estar | *ess-TAR* |

(See also "am," "is," "are," "was," "were," "been.")

beach	playa	*PLA-ya*
beans	frijoles (m)	*free-HO-lehs*
bear	oso	*OH-so*
beard	barba	*BAR-ba*
beautiful	bello	*BEL-yo*
beauty	belleza	*bel-YEH-sa*
beauty shop	salón de belleza (m)	*sa-LOHN deh bel-YEH-sa*
because	porque	*por-KEH*
bed	cama	*KA-ma*
bedroom	alcoba	*ahl-KO-ba*

bedspread	cubrecama (m)	*koo-breh-KA-ma*
beef	carne de res (f)	*KAR-neh deh rehs*
been (permanent status)	sido	*SEE-doh*
been (location or temporary status)	estado	*ess-TA-doh*
beer	cerveza	*sehr-VEH-sa*
before	antes	*AHN-tehs*
(to) begin	empezar	*em-peh-SAR*
behind	detrás	*deh-TRAHS*
(to) believe	creer	*kreh-EHR*
below	debajo	*deh-BA-ho*
belt	cinturón (m)	*seen-too-ROHN*
beside	al lado	*ahl LA-doh*
besides	además	*ah-deh-MAHS*
best (adj.)	el (la) mejor	*el (al) meh-HOR*
best (adv.)	lo mejor	*lo meh-HOR*
better	mejor	*meh-HOR*
between	entre	*EN-treh*
bicycle	bicicleta	*bee-see-KLEH-ta*
big	grande	*GRAHN-deh*
bill	cuenta	*KWEN-ta*
bird	pájaro	*PA-ha-ro*
birthday	cumple-años (m)	*koom-pleh-AHN-yohs*
black	negro	*NEH-gro*
blanket	frazada	*fra-SA-da*

blond	rubio	*ROO-b'yo*
blood	sangre (f)	*SAHN-greh*
blouse	blusa	*BLOO-sa*
blue	azul	*ah-SOOL*
boardinghouse	casa de huéspedes	*KA-sa deh WEHS-peh-dehs*
boat	barco	*BAR-ko*
body	cuerpo	*KWEHR-po*
Bolivia	Bolivia	*bo-LEEV-ya*
Bolivian	boliviano	*bo-leev-YA-no*
book	libro	*LEE-bro*
bookstore	librería	*lee-breh-REE-ya*
born	nacido	*na-SEE-doh*
(to) borrow	pedir prestado	*peh-DEER press-TA-doh*
boss	jefe	*HEH-feh*
both	ambos	*AHM-bohs*
(to) bother	molestar	*mo-less-TAR*
bottle	botella	*bo-TEL-ya*
bottom	fondo	*FOHN-doh*
bought	comprado	*kohm-PRA-doh*
boy	muchacho	*moo-CHA-cho*
brain	cerebro	*seh-REH-bro*
brake	freno	*FREH-no*
brave	valiente	*va-L'YEN-teh*
Brazil	Brasil	*bra-SEEL*
Brazilian	brasileño	*bra-see-LEN-yo*

bread	pan (m)	*pahn*
(to) break	romper	*rohm-PEHR*
breakfast	desayuno	*deh-sa-YOO-no*
(to) breathe	respirar	*res-pee-RAR*
bridge	puente (m)	*PWEN-teh*
briefcase	maletín (m)	*ma-leh-TEEN*
(to) bring	traer	*tra-EHR*
Bring me . . .	Tráigame . . .	*TRY-ga-meh . . .*
broken	roto	*RO-toh*
brother	hermano	*ehr-MA-no*
brother-in-law	cuñado	*koon-YA-doh*
brown	pardo, marrón	*PAR-doh, ma-ROHN*
brunette	morena	*mo-REH-na*
(to) build	construir	*kohn-stroo-EER*
building	edificio	*eh-dee-FEE-s'yo*
built	construído	*kohn-stroo-EE-doh*
bull	toro	*TOH-ro*
bullfight	corrida de toros	*ko-RREE-da deh TOH-rohs*
bullfighter	torero	*toh-REH-ro*
bullring	plaza de toros	*PLA-sa deh TOH-rohs*
bureau	cómoda	*KO-mo-da*
bus	autobús (m)	*ow-toh-BOOSS*
bus stop	parada de autobús	*pa-RA-da deh ow-toh-BOOSS*
business	negocio	*neh-GO-s'yo*
busy	ocupado	*oh-koo-PA-doh*

but	pero	*PEH-ro*
butter	mantequilla	*mahn-teh-KEEL-ya*
button	botón (m)	*bo-TOHN*
(to) buy	comprar	*kohm-PRAR*
by	por	*por*

C

cab	taxi (m)	*TAHX-see*
cabbage	**repollo**	*reh-POL-yo*
cable	cable (m)	*KA-bleh*
cake	torta	*TOR-ta*
(to) call	llamar	*l'ya-MAR*
Call me.	Llámeme.	*L'YA-meh-meh.*
camera	cámara	*KA-ma-ra*
can (to be able)	poder	*po-DEHR*
Can you . . . ?	¿Puede Ud. . . . ?	*¿PWEH-deh oo-STED . . . ?*
(I) can	puedo	*PWEH-doh*
(I) can't	no puedo	*no PWEH-doh*
can (container)	lata	*LA-ta*
can opener	abrelatas	*ah-breh-LA-tahs*
Canada	Canada	*KA-na-da*
Canadian	canadiense	*ka-na-d'YEN-seh*
candy	dulce (m)	*DOOL-seh*
cap	gorra	*GO-rra*
capable	capaz	*ka-PAHS*

cape	capa	*KA-pa*
captain	capitán (m)	*ka-pee-TAHN*
car	automóvil (m)	*ow-toh-MO-veel*
carburetor	carburador (m)	*kar-boo-ra-DOR*
card	tarjeta	*tar-HEH-ta*
(to take) care of	cuidar	*kwee-DAR*
(Be) careful!	¡Tenga cuidado!	*¡TEN-ga kwee-DA-doh!*
careless	descuidado	*des-kwee-DA-doh*
Caribbean	Caribe	*ka-REE-beh*
carrot	zanahoria	*sa-na-OHR-ya*
(to) carry	llevar	*l'yeh-VAR*
Carry this to . . .	Lleve esto a . . .	*L'YEH-veh ESS-toh ah . . .*
cashier	cajero	*ka-HEH-ro*
castle	castillo	*kahs-TEEL-yo*
cat	gato	*GA-toh*
cathedral	catedral (f)	*ka-teh-DRAHL*
Catholic	católico	*ka-TOH-lee-ko*
celebration	celebración (f)	*seh-leh-bra-S'YOHN*
cemetery	cementerio	*seh-men-TEH-r'yo*
cent	centavo	*sen-TA-vo*
center	centro	*SEN-tro*
century	siglo	*SEE-glo*
certainly	seguramente	*seh-goo-ra-MEN-teh*
certificate	certificado	*serh-tee-fee-KA-doh*
chair	silla	*SEEL-ya*

chandelier	araña	*ah-RAHN-ya*
change	cambio	*KAHM-b'yo*
(to) change	cambiar	*kahm-B'YAR*
charming	encantador	*en-kahn-ta-DOR*
chauffeur	chofer	*cho-FEHR*
cheap	barato	*ba-RA-toh*
check	cheque (m)	*CHEH-keh*
checkroom	guarda-ropa (m)	*gwahr-da-RRO-pa*
cheese	queso	*KEH-so*
chest	pecho	*PEH-cho*
chicken	pollo	*POHL-yo*
child	niño (m), niña (f)	*NEEN-yo, NEEN-ya*
Chile	Chile	*CHEE-leh*
Chilean	chileno	*chee-LEH-no*
China	China	*CHEE-na*
Chinese	chino	*CHEE-no*
chocolate	chocolate (m)	*cho-ko-LA-teh*
chop	chuleta	*choo-LEH-ta*
church	iglesia	*ee-GLEH-s'ya*
cigar	cigarro	*see-GA-rro*
cigarette	cigarrillo	*see-ga-REEL-yo*
city	ciudad (f)	*s'yoo-DAHD*
(to) clean	limpiar	*leem-P'YAR*
clear	claro	*KLA-ro*
clever	hábil	*AH-beel*
climate	clima (m)	*KLEE-ma*
close	cerca	*SEHR-ka*

(to) close	cerrar	*seh-RRAR*
closed	cerrado	*seh-RRA-doh*
clothes	ropa	*RO-pa*
coast	costa	*KO-sta*
coat	abrigo	*ah-BREE-go*
coffee	café (m)	*ka-FEH*
coin	moneda	*mo-NEH-da*
cold	frío	*FREE-yo*
college	universidad (f)	*oo-nee-vehr-see-DAHD*
Colombia	Colombia	*ko-LOHM-b'ya*
Colombian	colombiano	*ko-lohm-B'YA-no*
colonel	coronel (m)	*ko-ro-NEL*
color	color (m)	*ko-LOR*
(to) come	venir	*veh-NEER*
(I) come (am coming)	vengo	*VEN-go*
(you sg.) come (are coming)	(Ud.) viene	*V'YEH-neh*
(he, she) comes (is coming)	(él, ella) viene	*V'YEH-neh*
(we) come (are coming)	(nosotros) venimos	*veh-NEE-mohs*
(they, you pl.) come (are coming)	(ellos, ellas, Uds.) vienen	*V'YEH-nen*
Come!	¡Venga!	*¡VEN-ga!*
Come in!	¡Adelante!	*¡Ah-deh-LAHN-teh!*
(to) come back	volver	*vohl-VEHR*
comb	peine (m)	*PAY-neh*

company	compañía	*kohm-pahn-YEE-ya*
competition	competencia	*kohm-peh-TEN-s'ya*
complete	completo	*kohm-PLEH-toh*
computer	máquina calculadora	*MA-kee-na kahl-koo-la-DOH-ra*
concert	concierto	*kohn-S'YEHR-toh*
congratulations	felicitaciones (f)	*feh-lee-see-ta-S'YO-nehs*
conservative	conservador	*kohn-sehr-va-DOR*
(to) continue	continuar	*kohn-teen-WAHR*
conversation	conversación (f)	*kohn-vehr-sa-S'YOHN*
cook	cocinero	*ko-see-NEH-ro*
(to) cook	cocinar	*ko-see-NAR*
cool	fresco	*FRESS-ko*
copy	copia	*KO-p'ya*
corkscrew	sacacorchos (m)	*sa-ka-KOR-chohs*
corn	maíz (m)	*ma-EESS*
corner (street)	esquina	*ess-KEE-na*
corner (room)	rincón (m)	*reen-KOHN*
correct	correcto	*ko-RREK-toh*
(to) cost	costar	*kohs-TAR*
Costa Rica	Costa Rica	*KOHS-ta REE-ka*
Costa Rican	costarricense	*kohs-ta-rree-SEN-seh*
cotton	algodón (m)	*ahl-go-DOHN*
cough	tos (f)	*tohs*
could	poder	*po-DEHR*

Use the appropriate form of *poder* listed here, with the infinitive of the principal verb.

(I, you sg.**, he, she) could**	(yo, Ud., él ella) podría	*po-DREE-ah*
(we) could	podríamos	*po-DREE-ah-mohs*
(they, you pl.**) could**	podrían	*po-DREE-ahn*
country	país (m)	pa-EESS
cousin	primo	*PREE-mo*
cow	vaca	*VA-ka*
crab	cangrejo	*kahn-GREH-ho*
(to) crate	embalar	*em-ba-LAR*
crazy	loco	*LO-ko*
cream	crema	*KREH-ma*
(to) cross	cruzar	*kroo-SAR*
crossing	cruce (m)	*KROO-seh*
Cuba	Cuba	*KOO-ba*
Cuban	cubano	*koo-BA-no*
cup	taza	*TA-sa*
custom (habit)	costumbre (f)	*kohs-TOOM-breh*
customs (office)	aduana	*ah-DWA-na*
customs form	formulario de aduana	*for-moo-LA-r'yo deh ah-DWA-na*
(to) cut	cortar	*kor-TAR*

D

(to) dance	bailar	*by-LAR*
dangerous	peligroso	*peh-lee-GRO-so*
dark	oscuro	*ohs-KOO-ro*

darling	querido	*keh-REE-doh*
date (calendar)	fecha	*FEH-cha*
date (appointment)	cita	*SEE-ta*
daughter	hija	*EE-ha*
daughter-in-law	nuera	*NWEH-ra*
day	día (m)	*DEE-ya*
dead	muerto	*MWEHR-toh*
dear	querido	*keh-REE-doh*
December	diciembre	*dee-S'YEM-breh*
(to) decide	decidir	*deh-see-DEER*
deck (boat)	cubierta	*koo-B'YEHR-ta*
deep	hondo	*OHN-doh*
delay	demora	*deh-MO-ra*
delicious	delicioso	*deh-lee-S'YO-so*
delighted	encantado	*en-kahn-TA-doh*
dentist	dentista (m)	*den-TEESS-ta*
department store	tienda de departamentos	*T'YEN-da deh deh-par-ta-MEN-tohs*
desert	desierto	*deh-S'YEHR-toh*
desk	escritorio	*es-kree-TOR-yo*
dessert	postre (m)	*POHS-treh*
detour	desvío	*des-VEE-yo*
devil	diablo	*D'YA-blo*
dictionary	diccionario	*deek-s'yo-NA-r'yo*
different	diferente	*dee-feh-REN-teh*
difficult	difícil	*dee-FEE-seel*
(to) dine	cenar	*seh-NAR*

dining room	comedor (m)	*ko-meh-DOR*
dinner	cena	*SEH-na*
direction	dirección (f)	*dee-rek-S'YOHN*
dirty	sucio	*SOO-s'yo*
disappointed	desilusionado	*deh-see-loo-s'yo-NA-doh*
discount	descuento	*des-KWEN-toh*
divorced	divorciado	*dee-vor-S'YA-doh*
dizzy	mareado	*ma-reh-AH-doh*
(to) do	hacer	*ah-SEHR*

Do not translate the word "do" when it is used to make a question or a negative sentence in English. To ask a question in Spanish, put the subject after the verb, or simply make the sentence a question by the tone of your voice. To make a negative sentence, simply use **no** before the verb.

| Do you want . . . ? | ¿Quiere Ud. . . . ? | *¿K-YEH-reh oo-STED . . . ?* |

(**Don't** . . . use **sírvase no** with the verb. See p. 154 for usage.)

Don't you want . . . ?	¿No quiere . . . ?	*¿no K'YEH-reh . . . ?*
Don't do that!	¡sírvase no hacer eso!	*¡seer-va-seh no ah-SAIR EH-so!*
dock	muelle (m)	*MWEL-yeh*
doctor	médico	*MEH-dee-ko*
dog	perro	*PEH-rro*
dollar	dólar (m)	*DOH-lar*
door	puerta	*PWER-ta*
down	abajo	*ah-BA-ho*
downtown	el centro de la ciudad	*el SEN-tro deh la s'yoo-DAHD*

dress	vestido	*ves-TEE-doh*
(to) drink	beber	*beh-BEHR*
(to) drive	conducir	*kohn-doo-SEER*
driver	conductor	*kohn-dook-TOR*
driver's license	permiso de conducir	*pehr-MEE-so deh kohn-doo-SEER*
drugstore	farmacia	*far-MA-s'ya*
drunk	borracho	*bo-RRA-cho*
dry cleaner	tintorería	*teen-toh-reh-REE-ya*
duck	pato	*PA-toh*

E

each	cada	*KA-da*
ear (outer)	oreja	*oh-REH-ha*
ear (inner)	oído	*oh-EE-doh*
early	temprano	*tem-PRA-no*
(to) earn	ganar	*ga-NAR*
earth	tierra	*T'YEH-rra*
east	este	*ESS-teh*
easy	fácil	*FA-seel*
(to) eat	comer	*ko-MEHR*
egg	huevos	*WEH-vohs*
eight	ocho	*OH-cho*
eighteen	dieciocho	*d'yess-ee-OH-cho*
eight hundred	ochocientos	*oh-cho-S'YEN-tohs*
eighty	ochenta	*oh-CHEN-ta*
either, or	o	*oh*

either (one)	cualquiera	*kwahl-K'YEH-ra*
elbow	codo	*KO-doh*
electric	eléctrico	*eh-LEK-tree-ko*
elephant	elefante (m)	*eh-leh-FAHN-teh*
elevator	ascensor (m)	*ah-sen-SOR*
embarrassed	apenado	*ah-peh-NA-doh*
embassy	embajada	*em-ba-HA-da*
emergency	emergencia	*eh-mehr-HEN-s'ya*
employee	empleado	*em-pleh-AH-doh*
end	fin	*feen*
(to) end	terminar	*tehr-mee-NAR*
England	Englaterre	*een-gla-TEH-rra*
English	inglés (m), inglesa (f)	*een-GLEHSS een-GLEH-sa*
entertaining	divertido	*dee-vehr-TEE-doh*
error	error	*eh-RROR*
especially	especialmente	*ess-peh-s'yahl-MEN-teh*
Europe	Europa	*eh-oo-RO-pa*
European	europeo	*eh-oo-ro-PEH-oh*
even	aun	*ah-OON*
evening	noche (f)	*NO-cheh*
ever (sometime)	alguna vez	*ahl-GOO-na vess*
every	cada	*KA-da*
everybody	todo el mundo	*TOH-doh el MOON-doh*
everything	todo	*TOH-doh*
exactly	exactamente	*ek-sahk-ta-MEN-teh*

excellent	excelente	*ek-seh-LEN-teh*
except	excepto	*ek-SEP-toh*
(to) exchange	cambiar	*kahm-B'YAR*
Excuse me!	¡Perdón!	*¡pehr-DOHN!*
exit	salida	*sa-LEE-da*
expensive	caro	*KA-ro*
experience	experiencia	*es-peh-R'YEN-s'ya*
explanation	explicación (f)	*es-plee-ka-S'YOHN*
(to) export	exportar	*es-por-TAR*
extra	extra	*ES-tra*
eye	ojo	*OH-ho*

F

face	cara	*KA-ra*
factory	fábrica	*FA-bree-ka*
fair (show)	feria	*FEH-r'ya*
fall	caída	*ka-EE-da*
fall (autumn)	otoño	*oh-TOHN-yo*
(to) fall	caer	*ka-EHR*
family	familia	*fa-MEEL-ya*
famous	famoso	*fa-MO-so*
far	lejos	*LEH-hohs*
How far?	¿A qué distancia?	*¿ah keh-dees-TAHN-s'ya?*
fare	pasaje (m)	*pa-SA-heh*
farm	hacienda	*ah-S'YEN-da*
farther	más lejos	*mahs LEH-hohs*

fast	rápido	*RA-pee-doh*
fat	gordo	*GOR-doh*
father	padre (m)	*PA-dreh*
father-in-law	suegro	*SWEH-gro*
fax	fax	*fahks*
February	febrero	*feh-BREH-ro*
(to) feel	sentir	*sen-TEER*
fever	fiebre (f)	*F'YEH-breh*
few	pocos	*PO-kohs*
fifteen	quince	*KEEN-seh*
fifty	cincuenta	*seen-KWEN-ta*
(to) fight	luchar	*loo-CHAR*
(to) fill	llenar	*l'yeh-NAR*
film	película	*peh-LEE-koo-la*
finally	finalmente	*fee-nahl-MEN-teh*
(to) find	encontrar	*en-kohn-TRAR*
(to) find out	descubrir	*des-koo-BREER*
finger	dedo	*DEH-doh*
(to) finish	terminar	*tehr-mee-NAR*
finished	terminado	*tehr-mee-NA-doh*
fire	fuego	*FWEH-go*
first	primero	*pree-MEH-ro*
fish (in the water)	pez	*pess*
fish (on the plate)	pescado	*pess-KA-doh*
(to) fish	pescar	*pess-KAR*
five	cinco	*SEEN-ko*
flight	vuelo	*V'WEH-lo*
floor (of room)	suelo	*SWEH-lo*

floor (of a building)	piso	*PEE-so*
flower	flor (f)	*flor*
fly (insect)	mosca	*MOHS-ka*
(to) fly	volar	*vo-LAR*
food	comida	*ko-MEE-da*
foot	pie (m)	*p'yeh*
for (time or value)	por	*por*
for (use, purpose or destination)	para	*PA-ra*
foreigner	extranjero	*es-trahn-HEH-ro*
forest	selva	*SEL-va*
(to) forget	olvidar	*ohl-vee-DAR*
Don't forget!	¡No se olvide!	*¡no seh ohl-VEE-deh!*
fork	tenedor (m)	*teh-neh-DOR*
forty	cuarenta	*kwa-REN-ta*
fountain	fuente (f)	*FWEN-teh*
four	cuatro	*KWA-tro*
fourteen	catorce	*ka-TOR-seh*
fox	zorro	*SO-rro*
France	Francia	*FRAHN-s'ya*
free	libre	*LEE-breh*
French	francés (m), francesa (f)	*frahn-SEHS frahn-SEH-sa*
frequently	frecuentemente	*freh-kwen-teh-MEN-teh*
fresh	fresco	*FRES-ko*
Friday	viernes	*V'YEHR-ness*

fried	frito	*FREE-toh*
friend	amigo	*ah-MEE-go*
frog	rana	*RA-na*
from	desde	*DES-deh*
(in) front of	delante de	*deh-LAHN-teh deh*
fruit	fruta	*FROO-ta*
full	lleno	*L'YEH-no*
funny	gracioso	*gra-S'YO-so*
furniture	muebles (m)	*MWEH-blehs*
(in the) future	en el futuro	*en el foo-TOO-ro*
future tense	tiempo futuro	*TYEM-po foo-TOO-ro*

G

game	juego	*HWEH-go*
garage	garage (m)	*ga-RA-heh*
garden	jardín (m)	*har-DEEN*
gas	gas	*gahs*
gasoline	gasolina	*ga-so-LEE-na*
gas station	puesto de gasolina	*PWESS-toh deh ga-so-LEE-na*
general	general	*heh-neh-RAHL*
gentleman	caballero	*ka-bahl-YEH-ro*
German	alemán (m), alemana (f)	*ah-leh-MAHN ah-leh-MA-na*
Germany	Alemania	*ah-leh-MAHN-ya*
(to) get (to obtain)	conseguir	*kohn-seh-GHEER*

(to) get off	bajarse	*ba-HAR-seh*
(to) get on	subir	*soo-BEER*
(to) get out	salir	*sa-LEER*
Get out!	¡Fuera!	*¡FWEH-ra!*
(to) get up	levantarse	*leh-vahn-TAR-seh*
gift	regalo	*reh-GA-lo*
(to) give	dar	*dar*
Give me . . .	Deme . . .	*DEH-meh . . .*
girl	muchacha	*moo-CHA-cha*
glass (for windows)	vidrio	*VEE-dree-yo*
glass (drinking)	vaso	*VA-so*
glasses	lentes (m)	*LEN-tehs*
glove	guante (m)	*GWAHN-teh*
(to) go	ir	*eer*
(I) go (am going)	voy	*voy*
(you sg.**) go (are going)**	(Ud.) va	*va*
(he, she) goes (is going)	(él, ella) va	*va*
(we) go (are going)	vamos	*VA-mohs*
(they, you pl.**) go (are going)**	(ellos, ellas, Uds.) van	*vahn*
Go away!	¡Váyase!	*¡VA-ya-seh!*
(to) go away	irse	*EER-seh*
(to) go back	regresar	*reh-greh-SAR*
(to) go on	continuar	*kohn-teen-WAHR*
Go on!	¡Continúe!	*¡kohn-tee-NOO-eh!*

goat	cabra	*KA-bra*
God	Dios (m)	*d'yohs*
gold	oro	*OH-ro*
golf	golf (m)	*gohlf*
good	bueno	*BWEH-no*
goodbye	adiós	*ah-D'YOHS*
government	gobierno	*go-B'YEHR-no*
grandfather	abuelo	*ah-BWEH-lo*
grandmother	abuela	*ah-BWEH-la*
grandparents	abuelos	*ah-BWEH-los*
grapes	uvas	*OO-vahs*
grateful	agradecido	*ah-gra-deh-SEE-doh*
gray	gris	*greess*
great (before a noun)	gran	*grahn*
great (after a noun or alone)	grande	*GRAHN-deh*
Greece	Grecia	*GREH-s'ya*
Greek	griego	*GR'YEH-go*
green	verde	*VEHR-deh*
group	grupo	*GROO-po*
Guatemala	Guatemala	*gwa-teh-MA-la*
Guatemalan	Guatemalteco	*gwa-teh-mahl-TEH-ko*
guide	guía (m)	*GHEE-ya*
guitar	guitarra	*ghee-TA-rra*

H

hair	cabello	*ka-BEL-yo*
hairbrush	cepillo	*seh-PEEL-yo*
haircut	corte de pelo	*KOR-teh deh PEH-lo*
half	mitad (f)	*mee-TAHD*
half (adj.)	medio	*MEHD-yo*
hand	mano (f)	*MA-no*
happy	feliz	*feh-LEESS*
harbor	puerto	*PWEHR-toh*
hard	duro	*DOO-ro*
hat	sombrero	*sohm-BREH-ro*
(to) have (possess)	tener	*teh-NEHR*
(I) have	tengo	*TEN-go*
(you sg.**) have**	(Ud.) tiene	*T'YEN-neh*
(he, she) has	(él, ella) tiene	*T'YEH-neh*
(we) have	tenemos	*teh-NEH-mohs*
(they, you pl.**) have**	(ellos, ellas, Uds.) tienen	*T'YEH-nen*
Do you (sg.) **have . . . ?**	¿Tiene UD. . . . ?	*¿T'YEH-neh oo-STED . . . ?*
(to) have	haber	*ah-BEHR*

(Used to form the perfect tense; see p. 154.)

(I) have . . .	he . . .	*eh . . .*
(you sg.**) have . . .**	(Ud.) ha . . .	*ah . . .*
(he, she) has . . .	(él ella) ha . . .	*ah . . .*
(we) have . . .	hemos . . .	*EH-mohs . . .*

(they, you pl.**) have . . .**	(ellos, ellas, Uds.) han . . .	*ahn . . .*
he	él	*el*
head	cabeza	*ka-BEH-sa*
(to) hear	oír	*oh-EER*
heart	corazón (m)	*ko-ra-SOHN*
heavy	pesado	*peh-SA-doh*
Hello!	¡Hola!	*¡OH-la!*
(to) help	ayudar	*ah-yoo-DAR*
Help!	¡Socorro!	*¡so-KO-rro!*
her (dir. obj.)	la	*la*
(to) her	le	*leh*
her (adj.)	su	*soo*
here	aquí	*ah-KEE*
hers	el suyo, la suya	*el SOO-yo, la SOO-ya*
herself (reflex.)	se	*seh*
high	alto	*AHL-toh*
highway	carretera	*ka-rreh-TEH-ra*
hill	colina	*ko-LEE-na*
him (dir. obj.)	lo, le	*lo, leh*
(to) him	le	*leh*
himself (reflex.)	se	*seh*
his (adj.)	su	*soo*
his (pron.)	el suyo, la suya	*el SOO-yo, la SOO-ya*
history	historia	*ess-TOHR-ya*
holiday	día feriado	*DEE-yah feh-ree-YA-doh*

home	casa	*KA-sa*
(at) home	en casa	*en KA-sa*
Honduras	Honduras	*ohn-DOO-rahs*
Honduran	hondureño	*ohn-doo-REHN-yo*
(to) hope	esperar	*ess-peh-RAR*
horse	caballo	*ka-BAL-yo*
hospital	hospital (m)	*ohs-pee-TAHL*
hot	caliente	*ka-L'YEN-teh*
hotel	hotel (m)	*oh-TEL*
hour	hora	*OH-ra*
half hour	media hora	*MEHD-ya OH-ra*
house	casa	*KA-sa*
how	como	*KO-mo*
however	sin embargo	*seen em-BAR-go*
hundred	cien	*s'yen*
a hundred	ciento . . .	*S'YEN-toh . . .*
(to be) hungry	tener hambre	*teh-NEHR AHM-breh*
(to) hunt	cazar	*ka-SAHR*
(to) hurry	darse prisa	*DAR-seh PREE-sa*
Hurry up!	¡Dese prisa!	*¡DEH-seh PREE-sa!*
husband	esposo	*ess-PO-so*

I

I	yo	*yo*
ice	hielo	*YEH-lo*
ice cream	helado	*eh-LA-doh*

idiot	idiota (m)	*ee-D'YO-ta*
if	si	*see*
ill	enfermo	*en-FEHR-mo*
(to) import	importar	*eem-por-TAR*
important	importante	*eem-por-TAHN-teh*
impossible	imposible	*eem-po-SEE-bleh*
in	en	*en*
included	incluído	*een-kloo-EE-doh*
Indian	indio	*EEN-d'yo*
industry	industria	*een-DOOS-tree-ya*
information	información (f)	*een-for-ma-S'YOHN*
inhabitant	habitante (m)	*ah-bee-TAHN-teh*
inn	posada	*po-SA-da*
inquiry	pregunta	*preh-GOON-ta*
inside (direction)	adentro	*ah-DEN-tro*
inside (prep.)	dentro de	*DEN-tro deh*
instead	en vez de	*en vess deh*
intelligent	inteligente	*een-teh-lee-HEN-teh*
interested	interesado	*een-teh-reh-SA-doh*
interesting	interesante	*een-teh-reh-SAHN-teh*
interpreter	intérprete (m)	*een-TEHR-preh-teh*
into	dentro	*DEN-tro*
(to) introduce	presentar	*preh-sen-TAR*
invitation	invitación (f)	*een-vee-ta-S'YOHN*
Is (permanent status)	es	*ess*

is (location or temporary status)	está	*ess-TA*
(there) is	hay	*I*
island	isla	*ESS-la*
Israel	Israel	*ees-ra-EL*
Israeli	Israelí	*ees-ra-eh-LEE*
it (subject, or thing)	él (m), ella (f)	*el, EL-ya*
it (subject, referring to an idea or situation)	eso	*ES-so*
it (object)	lo (m), la (f)	*lo, la*
(indirect object)	le	*leh*
its	su	*soo*
Italian	italiano	*ee-tahl-YA-no*
Italy	Italia	*ee-TAHL-ya*

J

jacket	chaqueta	*cha-KEH-ta*
jail	cárcel (f)	*KAR-sel*
January	enero	*eh-NEH-ro*
Japan	Japón	*ha-POHN*
Japanese	japonés	*ha-po-NEHS*
jewelry	joyas	*HO-yahs*
Jew, Jewish	judío	*hoo-DEE-yo*
job	empleo	*em-PLEH-oh*
joke	chiste (m)	*CHEES-teh*

July	julio	*HOOL-yo*
June	junio	*HOON-yo*
just (only)	solamente	*so-la-MEN-teh*
just now	ahora mismo	*ah-OH-ra MEES-mo*

K

(to) keep	guardar	*gwahr-DAR*
Keep out!	¡No entre!	*¡no EN-treh!*
Keep quiet!	¡Cállese!	*¡KAHL-yeh-seh!*
key	llave (f)	*L'YA-veh*
kilogram	kilograma	*kee-lo-GRA-ma*
kilometer	kilómetro	*kee-LO-meh-tro*
kind (nice)	amable	*ah-MA-bleh*
kind (type)	tipo	*TEE-po*
king	rey	*ray*
kiss	beso	*BEH-so*
kitchen	cocina	*ko-SEE-na*
knee	rodilla	*ro-DEEL-ya*
knife	cuchillo	*koo-CHEEL-yo*
(to) know (a person)	conocer	*ko-no-SEHR*
Do you know (a person) . . . ?	¿Conoce a . . . ?	*¿ko-NO-seh ah . . .*
(to) know (a fact or how to)	sáber	*sa-BEHR*
Who knows?	¿Quién sabe?	*¿k'yen SA-beh?*

L

ladies' room	cuarto para señoras	*KWAHR-toh PA-ra sen-YO-rahs*
lady	dama	*DA-ma*
lake	lago	*LA-go*
lamb	cordero	*kor-DEH-ro*
land	tierra	*T'YEH-rra*
language	idioma (m)	*ee-D'YO-ma*
large	grande	*GRAHN-deh*
last	último	*OOL-tee-mo*
late	tarde	*TAR-deh*
later	más tarde	*mahs TAR-deh*
lawyer	abogado	*ah-bo-GA-doh*
(to) learn	aprender	*ah-pren-DEHR*
leather	cuero	*KWEH-ro*
(to) leave (something)	dejar	*deh-HAR*
(to) leave (depart)	salir	*sa-LEER*
left	izquierdo	*ees-K'YEHR-doh*
leg	pierna	*P'YEHR-na*
lemon	limón (m)	*lee-MOHN*
(to) lend	prestar	*press-TAR*
less	menos	*MEH-nohs*
lesson	lección (f)	*lek-S'YOHN*
let's	vamos a . . .	*VA-mohs ah . . .*
Let's go!	¡Vámonos!	*¡VA-mo-nohs!*
letter	carta	*KAR-ta*
lettuce	lechuga	*leh-CHOO-ga*

liberal	liberal	*lee-beh-RAHL*
liberty	libertad (f)	*lee-behr-TAHD*
lieutenant	teniente	*ten-YEN-teh*
life	vida	*VEE-da*
(to) lift	levantar	*leh-vahn-TAR*
light (weight)	liviano	*leev-YA-no*
light (illumination)	luz (f)	*looss*
like	como	*KO-mo*
Like this.	Así.	*ah-SEE*
(to) like	gustar	*goos-TAR*
(See page 81 for usage.)		
linen (material)	lino	*LEE-no*
lion	león	*leh-OHN*
lip	labio	*LAHB-yo*
list	lista	*LEES-ta*
(to) listen	escuchar	*es-koo-CHAR*
Listen!	¡Escuche!	¡es-KOO-cheh!
little (small)	pequeño	*peh-KEHN-yo*
a little	un poco	*oon PO-ko*
(to) live	vivir	*vee-VEER*
lived	vivido	*vee-VEE-doh*
living room	sala	*SA-la*
lobster	langosta	*lahn-GOHS-ta*
long	largo	*LAR-go*
(to) look	mirar	*mee-RAR*
Look!	¡Mire!	¡MEE-reh!
Look out!	¡Cuidado!	¡kwee-DA-doh!
loose	flojo	*FLO-ho*

(to) lose	perder	*pehr-DEHR*
losses	perdidas	*PEHR-dee-dahs*
lost	perdido	*pehr-DEE-doh*
lot (much)	mucho	*MOO-cho*
(to) love	querer	*keh-REHR*
low	bajo	*BA-ho*
luck	suerte (f)	*SWEHR-teh*
Good luck!	¡Buena suerte!	*¡BWEH-na SWEHR-teh!*
luggage	equipaje (m)	*eh-kee-PA-heh*
lunch	almuerzo	*ahl-MWEHR-so*

M

machine	máquina	*MA-kee-na*
madam	señora	*sen-YO-ra*
made	hecho	*EH-cho*
maid	criada	*kree-AH-da*
mailbox	buzón (m)	*boo-SOHN*
(to) make	hacer	*ah-SEHR*
man	hombre	*OHM-breh*
manager	gerente	*heh-REN-teh*
many	muchos	*MOO-chohs*
map	mapa (m)	*MA-pa*
March	marzo	*MAR-so*
market	mercado	*mehr-KA-doh*
married	casado	*ka-SA-doh*
Mass (religious)	misa	*MEE-sa*

matches	fósforos	*FOHS-fo-rohs*
May	mayo	*MA-yo*
maybe	quizás	*kee-SAHS*
May I?	¿Se puede?	*¿seh PWEH-deh?*
me	me	*meh*
(to) mean	querer decir	*keh-REHR deh-SEER*
meat	carne (f)	*KAR-neh*
mechanic	mecánico	*meh-KA-nee-ko*
medicine	medicina	*meh-dee-SEE-na*
Mediterranean	Mediterráneo	*meh-dee-teh-RRA-neh-oh*
(to) meet (encounter)	encontrar	*en-kohn-TRAR*
meeting	reunión (f)	*reh-oon-YOHN*
member	miembro	*M'YEM-bro*
(to) mend	remendar	*reh-men-DAR*
men's room	cuarto para caballeros	*KWAHR-toh PA-ra ka-bahl-YEH-rohs*
menu	menú	*meh-NOO*
message	mensaje (m)	*men-SA-heh*
meter (39.37 inches, slightly more than a yard)	metro	*MEH-tro*
Mexico	México	*MEH-hee-ko*
Mexican	Mexicano	*meh-hee-KA-no*
middle	medio	*MEHD-yo*
might See "could."		

mile	milla	*MEEL-ya*
milk	leche (f)	*LEH-cheh*
million	millón (m)	*meel-YOHN*
mine	el mío, la mía	*el MEE-yo, la MEE-ya*
mineral water	agua mineral	*AH-gwa mee-neh-RAHL*
minister	ministro	*mee-NEESS-tro*
minute	minuto	*mee-NOO-toh*
Miss	señorita	*sen-yo-REE-ta*
(to) miss (the train, etc.)	perder	*pehr-DEHR*
(to) miss (sentiment)	echar de menos	*eh-CHAR deh MEH-nohs*
mistake	error (m)	*eh-RROR*
misunderstanding	malentendido	*mahl-en-ten-DEE-doh*
model	modelo (m or f)	*mo-DEH-lo*
modern	moderno	*mo-DEHR-no*
moment	momento	*mo-MEN-toh*
Monday	lunes	*LOO-ness*
money	dinero	*dee-NEH-ro*
monkey	mono	*MO-no*
month	mes (m)	*mess*
monument	monumento	*mo-noo-MEN-toh*
moon	luna	*LOO-na*
more	más	*mahs*
morning	mañana	*mahn-YA-na*
mosquito	mosquito	*mohs-KEE-toh*
most	la mayor parte	*la ma-YOR PAR-teh*

mother	madre (f)	*MA-dreh*
mother-in-law	suegra	*SWEH-gra*
motor	motor (m)	*mo-TOR*
motorcycle	motocicleta	*mo-toh-see-KLEH-ta*
mountain	montaña	*mohn-TAHN-ya*
mouse	ratón (m)	*ra-TOHN*
mouth	boca	*BO-ka*
movie	película	*peh-LEE-koo-la*
movies	cine (m)	*SEE-neh*
Mr.	señor (Sr.)	*sen-YOR*
Mrs.	señora (Sra.)	*sen-YO-ra*
much	mucho	*MOO-cho*
museum	museo	*moo-SEH-oh*
music	música	*MOO-see-ka*
musician	músico	*MOO-see-ko*
must	hay que	*i keh*
(I, you, he, etc.) must go	hay que ir	*I keh eer*
mustache	bigote (m)	*bee-GO-teh*
mustard	mostaza	*mohs-TA-sa*
my	mi	*mee*
myself (reflex.)	me	*meh*

N

name	nombre (m)	*NOHM-breh*
napkin	servilleta	*sehr-veel-YEH-ta*
narcotics	narcóticos	*nar-KO-tee-kohs*

narrow	angosto	*ahn-GOHS-toh*
navy	marina	*ma-REE-na*
near	cerca	*SEHR-ka*
necessary	necesario	*neh-seh-SAR-yo*
neck	cuello	*KWEL-yo*
necktie	corbata	*kor-BA-ta*
(to) need	necesitar	*neh-seh-see-TAR*
neighborhood	vecindario	*veh-seen-DAR-yo*
nephew	sobrino	*so-BREE-no*
nervous	nervioso	*nehr-V'YO-so*
neutral	neutral	*neh-oo-TRAHL*
never	nunca	*NOON-ka*
Never mind.	No importa.	*no eem-POR-ta.*
new	nuevo	*NWEH-vo*
news	noticias	*no-TEE-s'yahs*
newspaper	periódico	*pehr-YO-dee-ko*
New Year	Año Nuevo	*AHN-yo NWEH-vo*
next	próximo	*PROHX-see-mo*
Nicaragua	Nicaragua	*nee-ka-RA-gwa*
Nicaraguan	nicaragüense	*nee-ka-ra-GWEN-seh*
nice	simpático	*seem-PA-tee-ko*
niece	sobrina	*so-BREE-na*
night	noche (f)	*NO-cheh*
nightclub	club nocturno	*kloob nohk-TOOR-no*
nightgown	camisa de dormir	*ka-MEE-sa deh dor-MEER*
nine	nueve	*NWEH-veh*

nineteen	diecinueve	*d'yess-ee-NWEH-veh*
ninety	noventa	*no-VEN-ta*
no	no	*no*
nobody	nadie	*NAHD-yeh*
noise	ruido	*RWEE-doh*
none	ninguno	*neen-GOO-no*
noon	mediodía (m)	*meh-d'yo-DEE-ya*
normal	normal	*nor-MAHL*
north	norte	*NOR-teh*
nose	nariz (f)	*na-REES*
not	no	*no*
not yet	todavía no	*to-da-VEE-ya no*
nothing	nada	*NA-da*
(to) notice	notar	*no-TAR*
noun	nombre (m)	*NOHM-breh*
November	noviembre	*no-V'YEM-breh*
now	ahora	*ah-OH-ra*
nowhere	en ninguna parte	*en neen-GOO-na PAR-teh*
number	número	*NOO-meh-ro*
nurse	enfermera	*en-fehr-MEH-ra*
nuts	nueces (f)	*NWEH-sehs*

O

occasionally	de vez en cuando	*deh vehs en KWAHN-doh*
occupation	ocupación	*oh-koo-pa-S'YOHN*
occupied	ocupado	*oh-koo-PA-doh*

ocean	océano	*oh-SEH-ah-no*
o'clock (See page 23 for usage.)		
October	octubre	*ohk-TOO-breh*
of	de	*deh*
(to) offer	ofrecer	*oh-freh-SEHR*
office	oficina	*oh-fee-SEE-na*
officer	oficial	*oh-fees-YAHL*
often	a menudo	*ah men-NOO-doh*
oil	aceite (m)	*ah-SAY-teh*
O.K.	está bien	*ess-TA b'yen*
old	viejo	*V'YEH-ho*
olive	aceituna	*ah-say-TOO-na*
omelet	tortilla de huevos	*tor-TEEL-ya deh WEH-vohs*
on	sobre	*SO-breh*
once	una vez	*OO-na vess*
At once!	¡En seguida!	*¡en seh-GHEE-da!*
one	uno	*OO-no*
one way (traffic)	una vía	*OO-na VEE-ya*
one way (ticket)	ida	*EE-da*
on time	a tiempo	*ah T'YEM-po*
onion	cebolla	*seh-BOHL-ya*
only	solamente	*so-la-MEN-teh*
open	abierto	*ah-B'YEHR-toh*
(to) open	abrir	*ah-BREER*
opera	ópera	*OH-peh-ra*
opinion	opinión (f)	*oh-peen-YOHN*

opportunity	oportunidad (f)	*oh-por-too-nee-DAHD*
opposite	opuesto	*oh-PWESS-toh*
or	o	*oh*
orange	naranja	*na-RAHN-ha*
orchestra	orquesta	*or-KESS-ta*
order	orden (f)	*OR-den*
(to) order	ordenar	*or-deh-NAR*
in order to	para	*PA-ra*
original	original	*oh-ree-hee-NAHL*
other	otro	*OH-tro*
ought to (I, you sg., he, she) ought to	debería (yo, Ud. él, élla)	*deh-beh-REE-ya*
(we) ought to	deberíamos	*deh-beh-REE-ya-mohs*
(they, you pl.) ought to	(ellos, ellas, Uds.) deberían	*deh-beh-REE-yahn*
our	nuestro	*NWESS-tro*
ours	el nuestro, la nuestra	*el NWESS-tro, la NWESS-tra*
ourselves (reflex.)	nos	*nohs*
outside	afuera	*ah-FWEH-ra*
over	encima	*en-SEE-ma*
over (finished)	terminado	*tehr-mee-NA-do*
overcoat	abrigo	*ah-BREE-go*
over there	allá	*ahl-YA*
overweight	sobrepeso	*so-breh-PEH-so*
(to) owe	deber	*deh-BEHR*
own	propio	*PRO-p'yo*

owner	dueño	*DWEN-yo*
ox	buey (m)	*bway*
oyster	ostra	*OHS-tra*

P

package	paquete (m)	*pa-KEH-teh*
paid	pagado	*pa-GA-doh*
pain	dolor (m)	*doh-LOR*
(to) paint	pintar	*peen-TAR*
painting	cuadro	*KWA-dro*
palace	palacio	*pa-LA-s'yo*
pan	cacerola	*ka-seh-RO-la*
Panama	Panamá	*pa-na-MA*
Panamanian	panameño	*pa-na-MEN-yo*
paper	papel (m)	*pa-PEL*
parade	desfile (m)	*des-FEE-leh*
Paraguay	Paraguay	*pa-ra-G'WY*
Paraguayan	paraguayo	*pa-ra-GWA-yo*
Pardon me!	¡Perdón!	*¡pehr-DOHN!*
park	parque (m)	*PAR-keh*
(to) park	estacionar	*ess-ta-s'yo-NAR*
parents	padres	*PA-drehs*
part	parte (f)	*PAR-teh*
participle	participio	*par-tee-SEEP-yo*
partner	socio	*SOHS-yo*
party	fiesta	*F'YES-ta*
passenger	pasajero	*pa-sa-HEH-ro*

passport	pasaporte (m)	*pa-sa-POR-teh*
past	pasado	*pa-SA-doh*
past tense	tiempo pasado	*T'YEM-po pa-SA-doh*
(to) pay	pagar	*pa-GAR*
(to) pay cash	pagar al contado	*pa-GAR ahl kohn-TA-doh*
peace	paz (f)	*pahss*
pen	pluma	*PLOO-ma*
pencil	lápiz (m)	*LA-peess*
people	gente (f)	*HEN-teh*
percent	por ciento	*por S'YEN-toh*
perfect	perfecto	*pehr-FEK-toh*
perfume	perfume (m)	*pehr-FOO-meh*
perhaps	quizás	*kee-SAHS*
permanent	permanente	*pehr-ma-NEN-teh*
(to) permit	permitir	*pehr-mee-TEER*
permitted	permitido	*pehr-mee-TEE-doh*
person	persona	*pehr-SO-na*
Peru	Perú (m)	*peh-ROO*
Peruvian	Peruano	*peh-RWA-no*
Philippines	Filipinas	*fee-lee-PEE-nahs*
phone	teléfono	*teh-LEH-fo-no*
photo	foto (f)	*FO-toh*
piano	piano	*P'YA-no*
(to) pick up	recoger	*reh-ko-HEHR*
picture	retrato	*reh-TRA-toh*
piece	pedazo	*peh-DA-so*
pier	muelle (m)	*MWEL-yeh*

pill	píldora	*PEEL-doh-ra*
pillow	almohada	*ahl-mo-AH-da*
pin	alfiler (m)	*ahl-fee-LEHR*
pink	rosado	*ro-SA-doh*
pipe	pipa	*PEE-pa*
pistol	pistola	*pees-TOH-la*
place	lugar (m)	*loo-GAR*
plain (simple)	sencillo	*sen-SEEL-yo*
plan	plan (m)	*plahn*
plane	avión (m)	*ahv-YOHN*
planet	planeta (m)	*pla-NEH-ta*
plant (garden)	planta	*plahn-ta*
plant (factory)	fábrica	*FA-bree-ka*
plate	plato	*PLA-toh*
play (theater)	pieza	*P'YEH-sa*
(to) play	jugar	*hoo-GAR*
plastic	plástico	*PLAHS-tee-ko*
pleasant	agradable	*ah-gra-DA-bleh*
please	por favor	*por fa-VOR*
pleasure	placer (m)	*pla-SEHR*
plural	plural (m)	*ploo-RAHL*
pocket	bolsillo	*bol-SEEL-yo*
poetry	poesía	*po-eh-SEE-ya*
(to) point	señalar	*sen-ya-LAHR*
poisonous	venenoso	*veh-neh-NO-so*
police	policía (f)	*po-lee-SEE-ya*
policeman	policía (m)	*po-lee-SEE-ya*

police station	cuartel de policía (m)	*kwahr-TEL deh po-lee-SEE-ya*
polite	cortés-	*kor-TEHS*
poor	pobre	*PO-breh*
pope	papa (m)	*PA-pa*
popular	popular	*po-poo-LAR*
pork	cerdo	*SEHR-doh*
Portugal	Portugal	*por-too-GAHL*
Portuguese	portugués	*por-too-GAYSS*
possible	posible	*po-SEE-bleh*
postcard	tarjeta postal	*tar-HEH-ta pos-TAHL*
post office	correo	*ko-RREH-yo*
potato	papa	*PA-pa*
pound	libra	*LEE-bra*
(to) practice	practicar	*prahk-tee-KAR*
(to) prefer	preferir	*preh-feh-REER*
pregnant	embarazada	*em-bar-ra-SA-da*
(to) prepare	preparar	*preh-pa-RAR*
present (time)	presente	*preh-SEN-teh*
present (gift)	regalo	*reh-GA-lo*
president	presidente (m)	*preh-see-DEN-teh*
(to) press (clothes)	planchar	*plahn-CHAR*
pretty	bonito	*bo-NEE-toh*
previously	previamente	*prehv-ya-MEN-teh*
price	precio	*PREH-s'yo*
priest	sacerdote	*sa-sehr-DOH-teh*
prince	príncipe	*PREEN-see-peh*
princess	princesa	*preen-SEH-sa*

principal	principal	*preen-see-PAHL*
prison	cárcel (f)	*KAR-sel*
private	privado	*pree-VA-doh*
probably	probablemente	*pro-ba-bleh-MEN-teh*
problem	problema (m)	*pro-BLEH-ma*
production	producción (f)	*pro-dook-S'YOHN*
profession	profesión (f)	*pro-feh-S'YOHN*
professor	profesor (m)	*pro-feh-SOR*
profits	beneficios	*beh-neh-FEE-s'yohs*
program	programa (m)	*pro-GRA-ma*
(to) promise	prometer	*pro-meh-TEHR*
promised	prometido	*pro-meh-TEE-doh*
pronoun	pronombre (m)	*pro-NOHM-breh*
(to) pronounce	pronunciar	*pro-noon-S'YAR*
propaganda	propaganda	*pro-pa-GAHN-da*
property	propiedad (f)	*prop-yeh-DAHD*
Protestant	protestante	*pro-tess-TAHN-teh*
public	público	*POO-blee-ko*
publicity	publicidad (f)	*poo-blee-see-DAHD*
publisher	editor (m)	*eh-dee-TOR*
(to) pull	tirar	*tee-RAR*
(to) purchase	comprar	*kohm-PRAR*
pure	puro	*POO-ro*
purple	morado	*mo-RA-doh*
purse	cartera	*kar-TEH-ra*
(to) push	empujar	*em-poo-HAR*

| **(to) put** | poner | *po-NEHR* |
| **(to) put on** | ponerse | *po-NEHR-seh* |

Q

quality	calidad (f)	*ka-lee-DAHD*
queen	reina	*RAY-na*
question	pregunta	*preh-GOON-ta*
quick	rápido	*RA-pee-doh*
quickly	rápidamente	*RA-pee-da-MEN-teh*
quiet	callado	*kahl-YA-doh*
quite	bastante	*ba-STAHN-teh*

R

rabbi	rabino	*ra-BEE-no*
rabbit	conejo	*ko-NEH-ho*
race (contest)	carrera	*ka-REEH-ra*
race (ethnic)	raza	*RA-sa*
radio	radio	*RAH-d'yo*
railroad	ferrocarril (m)	*feh-rro-ka-RREEL*
rain	lluvia	*L'YOOV-ya*
It's raining.	Está lloviendo.	*ess-TA l'yo-V'YEN-doh*
raincoat	impermeable	*eem-pehr-meh-AH-bleh*
rapidly	rápidamente	*RA-pee-da-MEN-teh*

rarely	rara vez	*RA-ra vess*
rate	cantidad (f)	*kahn-tee-DAHD*
rather	más bien	*mahs b'yen*
(I, he, she, you) would rather	preferiría	*preh-feh-ree-REE-ya*
razor	navaja de afeitar	*na-VA-ha deh ah-fay-TAR*
(to) read	leer	*leh-EHR*
ready	listo	*LEES-toh*
really	verdaderamente	*vehr-da-deh-ra-MEN-teh*
reason	razón (f)	*ra-SOHN*
receipt	recibo	*reh-SEE-bo*
(to) receive	recibir	*reh-see-BEER*
recently	recientemente	*rehs-yen-teh-MEN-teh*
recipe	receta	*reh-SEH-ta*
(to) recognize	reconocer	*reh-ko-no-SEHR*
(to) recommend	recomendar	*reh-ko-men-DAR*
red	rojo	*RO-ho*
refrigerator	nevera	*neh-VEH-ra*
(to) refuse	rehusar	*reh-oo-SAR*
(my) regards to . . .	(mis) recuerdos a . . .	*meess reh-KWER-dohs ah . . .*
regular	regular	*reh-goo-LAR*
religion	religión (f)	*reh-lee-H'YOHN*
(to) remain	quedarse	*keh-DAR-seh*
(to) remember	recordar	*reh-kor-DAR*
(to) rent	alquilar	*ahl-kee-LAR*
(to) repair	reparar	*reh-pa-RAR*

(to) repeat	repetir	*reh-peh-TEER*
Repeat, please!	¡Repita, por favor!	*¡reh-PEE-ta, por fa-VOR!*
report	reporte (m)	*reh-POR-teh*
(to) represent	representar	*reh-preh-sen-TAR*
representative	representante (m)	*reh-preh-sen-TAHN-teh*
resident (m or f)	residente	*reh-see-DEN-teh*
responsible	responsable	*rehs-pohn-SA-bleh*
rest (remainder)	resto	*RESS-toh*
(to) rest	descansar	*des-kahn-SAR*
restaurant	restaurante (m)	*rest-ow-RAHN-teh*
(to) return (to a place)	regresar	*reh-greh-SAR*
(to) return (give back)	devolver	*deh-vohl-VEHR*
revolution	revolución (f)	*reh-vo-loo-S'YOHN*
reward	recompensa	*reh-kohm-PEN-sa*
rice	arroz (m)	*ah-RROHS*
rich	rico	*REE-ko*
(to) ride (a horse, bicycle, etc.)	montar a	*mohn-TAR ah*
right (direction)	derecho	*deh-REH-cho*
to the right	a la derecha	*ah lah deh-REH-cha*
right (correct)	correcto	*ko-RREK-toh*
You're right.	Tiene razón.	*T'YEH-neh ra-SOHN.*
Right away!	¡En seguida!	*¡en seh-GHEE-da!*
ring	anillo	*ah-NEEL-yo*

riot	motín (m)	*mo-TEEN*
river	río	*REE-yo*
road	camino	*ka-MEE-no*
roof	techo	*TEH-cho*
room	cuarto	*KWAHR-toh*
room (space)	espacio	*eh-SPA-s'yo*
room service	servicio de comedor	*sehr-VEE-s'yo deh ko-meh-DOR*
round trip	ida y vuelta	*EE-da ee VWEL-ta*
route	ruta	*ROO-ta*
rug	alfombra	*ahl-FOHM-bra*
rum	ron	*rohn*
(to) run	correr	*ko-RREHR*
Run!	¡Corra!	*¡KO-rra!*
Russia	Rusia	*ROO-s'ya*
Russian	ruso	*ROO-so*

S

sad	triste	*TREESS-teh*
safe (adj.)	seguro	*seh-GOO-ro*
safety pin	imperdible (m)	*eem-pehr-DEE-bleh*
said	dicho	*DEE-cho*
sailor	marinero	*ma-ree-NEH-ro*
saint (Generally shortened to *San* before masculine names.)	santo (m), santa (f)	*SAHN-toh, SAHN-ta*

salad	ensalada	*en-sa-LA-da*
salary	sueldo	*SWEL-doh*
sale	venta	*VEN-ta*
Salvador	Salvador	*sahl-va-DOR*
Salvadorian	salvadoreño	*sahl-va-doh-REHN-yo*
same	mismo	*MEES-mo*
sandwich	emparedado	*em-pa-reh-DA-doh*
Saturday	sábado	*SA-ba-doh*
(to) say	decir	*deh-SEER*
scenery	paisaje (m)	*py-SA-heh*
school	escucla	*ess-KWEH-la*
science	ciencia	*S'YEN-s'ya*
scientist	scientífico	*s'yen-TEE-fee-ko*
scissors	tijeras	*tee-HEH-rahs*
Scot	escocés	*ess-ko-SESS*
Scotland	Escocia	*ess-Ko-s'ya*
sea	mar (m)	*mar*
seafood	mariscos	*ma-REES-kohs*
season	estación (f)	*ess-ta-S'YOHN*
seat	asiento	*ah-S'YEN-toh*
secretary	secretaria (f)	*seh-kreh-TAR-ya*
(to) see	ver	*vehr*
(to) seem	parecer	*pa-reh-SEHR*
It seems . . .	Parece . . .	*pa-REH-seh . . .*
seen	visto	*VEES-toh*
seldom	rara vez	*RA-ra vess*
self (my, you, him, her)	(yo, Ud., él, ella) mismo	*MEESS-mo*

(to) sell	vender	*ven-DEHR*
(to) send	mandar	*mahn-DAR*
(to) send for	enviar por	*en-vee-AR por*
separate (adj.)	separado	*seh-pa-RA-doh*
separate (v.)	separar	*seh-pa-RAR*
September	septiembre	*sep-T'YEM-breh*
serious	serio	*SEHR-yo*
service	servicio	*sehr-VEE-s'yo*
seven	siete	*SE'YEH-teh*
seventeen	diecisiete	*d'yess-ee-S'YEH-teh*
seventy	setenta	*seh-TEN-ta*
several	varios	*VAR-yohs*
shall (See "will.")		
shampoo	shampú (m)	*shahm-POO*
shark	tiburón (m)	*tee-boo-ROHN*
sharp	agudo	*ah-GOO-doh*
she	ella	*EL-ya*
ship	barco	*BAR-ko*
shipment	envío	*en-VEE-yo*
shirt	camisa	*ka-MEE-sa*
shoe	zapato	*sa-PA-toh*
shop	tienda	*T'YEN-da*
short	corto	*KOR-toh*
should	deber	*deh-BEHR*

(Use the appropriate forms of *deber* with the infinitive.)

(I, you, sg., **he, she) should**	debería	deh-beh-RRE-ya
(we) should	deberíamos	*deh-beh-REE-ya-mohs*

(they, you pl.**) should**	deberían	*deh-beh-REE-yahn*
shoulder	hombro	*OHM-bro*
show	espectáculo	*ess-pek-TA-koo-lo*
(to) show	mostrar	*mohs-TRAR*
Show me!	¡Muéstreme!	*¡MWESS-treh-meh!*
shower	ducha	*DOO-cha*
shrimps	camarones (m)	*ka-ma-RO-nehs*
shut	cerrado	*seh-RRA-doh*
(to) shut	cerrar	*seh-RRAR*
sick	enfermo	*en-FEHR-mo*
(to) sign	firmar	*feer-MAR*
silk	seda	*SEH-da*
silver	plata	*PLA-ta*
simple	sencillo	*sen-SEEL-yo*
since	desde	*DEHS-deh*
sincerely	sinceramente	*seen-seh-ra-MEN-teh*
(to) sing	cantar	*kahn-TAR*
singer (m or f)	cantante	*kahn-TAHN-teh*
sir	señor	*sen-YOR*
sister	hermana	*ehr-MA-na*
sister-in-law	cuñada	*koon-YA-da*
(to) sit down	sentarse	*sen-TAR-seh*
Sit down!	¡Siéntese!	*¡S'YEN-teh-seh!*
six	seis	*sayss*
sixteen	dieciseis	*d'yess-ee-SAYSS*
sixty	sesenta	*seh-SEN-ta*

size	tamaño	*ta-MAHN-yo*
(to) skate	patinar	*pa-tee-NAR*
(to) ski	esquiar	*ess-kee-AR*
skin	piel (f)	*p'yell*
skirt	falda	*FAHL-da*
sky	cielo	*S'YEH-lo*
(to) sleep	dormir	*dor-MEER*
sleeve	manga	*MAHN-ga*
slowly	despacio	*dess-PA-s'yo*
small	pequeño	*peh-KEN-yo*
smoke	humo	*OO-mo*
(to) smoke	fumar	*foo-MAR*
snow	nieve (f)	*N'YEH-veh*
so	así	*ah-SEE*
soap	jabón (m)	*ha-BOHN*
sock	media	*MEHD-ya*
sofa	sofá (m)	*so-FA*
soft	blando	*BLAHN-doh*
soldier	soldado	*sol-DA-doh*
some (a little)	un poco de	*oon PO-ko deh*
some (adj.)	algunos	*ahl-GOO-nohs*
somebody	alguien	*AHL-g'yen*
something	algo	*AHL-go*
something else	algo más	*AHL-go mahs*
sometimes	algunas veces	*ahl-GOO-nahs VEH-sehs*
somewhere	en alguna parte	*en ahl-GOO-na PAR-teh*
son	hijo	*EE-ho*

son-in-law	yerno	*YEHR-no*
song	canción (f)	*kahn-S'YOHN*
soon	pronto	*PROHN-toh*
(I am) sorry.	Lo siento	*lo S'YEN-toh*
soup	sopa	*SO-pa*
south	sur	*soor*
South America	Sur América	*soor ah-MEH-ree-ka*
South American	Suramericano	*soor-ah-meh-ree-KA-no*
souvenir	recuerdo	*reh-KWER-doh*
Spain	España	*ess-PAHN-ya*
Spanish, Spaniard	español	*ess-pahn-YOHL*
(to) speak	hablar	*ah-BLAR*
special	especial	*ess-peh-S'YAHL*
(to) spend	gastar	*gahs-TAR*
spoon	cuchara	*koo-CHA-ra*
sport	deporte (m)	*deh-POR-teh*
spring (season)	primavera	*pree-ma-VEH-ra*
stairs	escalera	*ess-ka-LEH-ra*
stamp	estampilla	*ess-tahm-PEEL-ya*
star	estrella	*ess-TREL-ya*
(to) start	empezar	*em-peh-SAR*
state	estado	*ess-TA-doh*
station	estación (f)	*ess-ta-S'YOHN*
statue	estatua	*ess-TA-twah*
(to) stay	quedarse	*keh-DAR-seh*
steak	bistec (m)	*beess-TEK*
steel	acero	*ah-SEH-ro*

stewardess	aeromoza	*ah-eh-ro-MO-sa*
still (adv.)	todavía	*toh-da-VEE-ya*
stocking	media	*MEHD-ya*
stockmarket	bolsa	*BOHL-sa*
stocks (shares)	acciones	*ahk-S'YOH-nehs*
stone	piedra	*P'YEH-dra*
Stop!	¡Pare!	*¡PA-reh!*
Stop it!	¡Deje de hacer eso!	*¡DEH-heh deh ah-SEHR EH-so!*
store	tienda	*T'YEN-da*
storm	tormenta	*tor-MEN-ta*
story	cuento	*KWEN-toh*
straight or **straight ahead**	derecho	*deh-REH-cho*
strange	extraño	*es-TRAHN-yo*
street	calle (f)	*KAHL-yeh*
string	cuerda	*KWER-da*
strong	fuerte	*FWEHR-teh*
student (m or f)	estudiante	*ess-too-D'YAHN-teh*
(to) study	estudiar	*ess-too-D'YAR*
style	estilo	*ess-TEE-lo*
subway	metro, subterráneo (in Spain)	*MEH-tro, soob-teh-RRA-neh-yo*
suddenly	de repente	*deh reh-PEN-teh*
suede	gamuza	*ga-MOO-sa*
sugar	azúcar (f)	*ah-SOO-kar*
suit (clothes)	traje (m)	*TRA-heh*
suitcase	maleta	*ma-LEH-ta*

summer	verano	*veh-RA-no*
sun	sol (m)	*sohl*
Sunday	domingo	*do-MEEN-go*
sure	seguro	*seh-GOO-ro*
surely	seguramente	*seh-goo-ra-MEN-teh*
surprise	sorpresa	*sor-PREH-sa*
sweater	suéter (m)	*SWEH-tehr*
sweet	dulce	*DOOL-seh*
(to) swim	nadar	*na-DAR*
swimming pool	piscina	*pee-SEE-na*
Swiss	suizo	*SWEE-so*
Switzerland	Suiza	*SWEE-sa*

T

tablecloth	mantel (m)	*mahn-TEL*
tailor	sastre (m)	*SAHS-treh*
(to) take	tomar	*toh-MAR*
(to) take away	llevarse	*l'yeh-VAR-seh*
(to) take a walk (or a ride)	dar un paseo	*dar oon pa-SEH-oh*
(to) talk	hablar	*ah-BLAR*
tall	alto	*AHL-toh*
tank	tanque (m)	*TAHN-keh*
tape	cinta	*SEEN-ta*
tape recorder	grabador (m)	*gra-ba-DOR*
tax	impuesto	*eem-PWESS-toh*

taxi	taxi (m)	*TAHX-see*
tea	té (m)	*teh*
(to) teach	enseñar	en-sen-YAR
teacher	maestro	*ma-ESS-tro*
team	equipo	*eh-KEE-po*
telegram	telegrama (m)	*teh-leh-GRA-ma*
telephone	teléfono	*teh-LEH-fo-no*
television	televisión (f)	*teh-leh-vee-S'YOHN*
(to) tell	decir	*deh-SEER*
Tell him (her) that . . .	Dígale que . . .	*DEE-ga-leh keh . . .*
temperature	temperatura	*tem-peh-ra-TOO-ra*
temple	templo	*TEM-plo*
ten	diez	*d'yess*
tennis	tenis (m)	*TEH-neess*
terrace	teraza	*teh-RRA-sa*
terrible	terrible	*teh-RREE-bleh*
than (Before a number use *de.*)	que	*keh*
Thank you.	Gracias.	*GRA-s'yahs.*
that (pron.)	ése (m), ésa (f)	*ESS-eh, ESS-ah*
that (neut.)	eso	*ES-so*
that (adj.)	ese, esa	*ESS-eh, ESS-ah*
that (rel. pron. or conj.)	que	*keh*
the	el (m)	*el*
	la (f)	*lah*
	los (m. pl.)	*lohs*
	las (f. pl.)	*lahs*

their	su	*soo*
theirs	el suyo (m), la suya (f)	*el SOO-yo, la SOO-ya*
them	los (m), las (f)	*lohs, lahs*
themselves (reflex.)	se	*seh*
then	entonces	*en-TOHN-sess*
there	allí	*ahl-YEE*
There is . . .	Hay . . .	*I*
There are . . .	Hay . . .	*I*
these (pronoun)	éstos (m), éstas (f)	*ESS-tohs, ESS-tahs*
these (adjective)	estos (m), estas (f)	*ESS-tohs, ESS-tahs*
they	ellos (m), ellas (f)	*EL-yohs, EL-yahs*
thin	delgado	*del-GA-doh*
thing	cosa	*KO-sa*
(to) think	pensar	*pen-SAR*
Do you think that . . . ?	¿Piensa Ud. que . . . ?	*¿P'YEN-sa oo-STED keh . . . ?*
I think	Pienso que . . .	*P'YEN-so keh . . .*
third	tercero	*tehr-SEH-ro*
(to be) thirsty	tener sed	*teh-NEHR sed*
thirteen	trece	*TREH-seh*
thirty	treinta	*TRAIN-ta*
this (pron.)	éste (m), ésta (f)	*ESS-teh, ESS-tah*
this (adj.)	este (m), esta (f)	*ESS-teh, ESS-ta*
those (pron.)	ésos (m), ésas (f)	*ESS-ohs, ESS-ahs*
those (adj.)	esos (m), esas (f)	*ESS-ohs, ESS-ahs*
thousand	mil	*meel*
thread	hilo	*EE-lo*

three	tres	*trehs*
throat	garganta	*gahr-GAHN-ta*
through	por	*por*
Thursday	jueves	*HWEH-vehs*
ticket	billete (m)	*beel-YEH-teh*
tie	corbata	*kor-BA-ta*
tiger	tigre (m)	*TEE-greh*
time	tiempo	*T'YEM-po*
tip	propina	*pro-PEE-na*
tire	llanta	*L'YAHN-ta*
tired	cansado	*kahn-SA-doh*
to (direction)	a	*ah*
to (in order to)	para	*PA-ra*
tobacco	tabaco	*ta-BA-ko*
today	hoy	*oy*
toe	dedo del pie	*DEH-do del p'yeh*
together	juntos	*HOON-tohs*
toilet	excusado	*ess-koo-SA-doh*
tomato	tomate (m)	*toh-MA-teh*
tomb	tumba	*TOOM-ba*
tongue	lengua	*LEN-gwa*
tonight	esta noche	*ESS-ta NO-cheh*
too (also)	también	*tahm-B'YEN*
too (excessive)	demasiado	*deh-ma-S'YA-doh*
tool	herramienta	*eh-rra-M'YEN-ta*
tooth (front)	diente (m)	*D'YEN-teh*
tooth (molar)	muela	*MWEH-la*

toothbrush	cepillo de dientes	*seh-PEEL-yo deh D'YEN-tehs*
toothpaste	pasta de dientes	*PAHS-ta deh, D'YEN-tehs*
tour	jira	*HEE-ra*
tourist (m or f)	turista	*too-REESS-ta*
toward	hacia	*AHS-ya*
towel	toalla	*toh-AHL-ya*
tower	torre (f)	*TOH-rreh*
town	pueblo	*PWEH-blo*
toy	juguete (m)	*hoo-GHEH-teh*
traffic	tránsito	*TRAHN-see-toh*
train	tren (m)	*trehn*
translation	traducción (f)	*tra-dook-S'YOHN*
(to) travel	viajar	*v'ya-HAR*
travel agent	agente de viajes	*ah-HEN-teh deh V'YA-hehs*
traveler	viajero	*v'ya-HEH-ro*
treasurer	tesorero	*teh-so-REH-ro*
tree	árbol (m)	*AR-bohl*
trip	viaje (m)	*V'YA-heh*
trouble	problema (m)	*pro-BLEH-ma*
trousers	pantalones (m)	*pahn-ta-LO-nehs*
truck	camión (m)	*kah-M'YOHN*
true	verdad	*vehr-DAHD*
truth	verdad (f)	*vehr-DAHD*
(to) try	tratar	*tra-TAR*
(to) try on	probarse	*pro-BAR-seh*
Tuesday	martes	*MAR-tehs*

Turkey	Turquía	*toor-KEE-ya*
Turkish	turco	*TOOR-ko*
(to) turn	voltear	*vohl-teh-AR*
(to) turn off	apagar	*ah-pa-GAR*
(to) turn on	poner	*po-NEHR*
twelve	doce	*DOH-seh*
twenty	veinte	*VAIN-teh*
two	dos	*dohs*
typewriter	máquina de escribir	*MA-kee na deh ess-kree-BEER*
typical	típico	*TEE-pee-ko*

U

ugly	feo	*FEH-oh*
umbrella	paraguas (m)	*pa-RA-gwahs*
uncle	tío	*TEE-yo*
under	debajo de	*deh-BA-ho deh*
underneath	debajo	*deh-BA-ho*
understand	comprender	*kohm-pren-DEHR*
Do you understand?	¿Comprende Ud.?	*¿kohm-PREN-deh oo-STED?*
I don't understand.	No comprendo.	*no kohm-PREN-doh.*
underwear	ropa interior	*RO-pa een-tehr-YOR*
unfortunately	desafortunadamente	*dehs-ah-for-too-na-da-MEN-teh*
uniform	uniforme (m)	*oo-nee-FOR-meh*

United Nations	Naciones Unidas	*na-S'YO-nehss oo-NEE-dahs*
United States	Estados Unidos	*ess-TA-dohs oo-NEE-dohs*
university	universidad (f)	*oo-nee-vehr-see-DAHD*
until	hasta	*AHS-ta*
up	arriba	*ah-RREE-ba*
urgent	urgente	*oor-HEN-teh*
Uruguay	Uruguay (m)	*oo-roo-G'WY*
Uruguayan	uruguayo	*oo-roo-GWA-yo*
us	nos	*nohs*
(to) use	usar	*oo-SAR*
used to (in the habit of)	acostumbrado a	*ah-kohs-toom-BRA-doh ah*
useful	útil	*OO-teel*
usually	usualmente	*oo-swahl-MEN-teh*

V

vacant	desocupado	*dehs-oh-koo-PA-doh*
vacation	vacación (f)	*va-ka-S'YOHN*
vaccination	vacuna	*va-KOO-na*
valley	valle (m)	*VAHL-yeh*
valuable	valioso	*va-L'YO-so*
value	valor (m)	*va-LOR*
vanilla	vainilla	*vy-NEEL-ya*
various	varios	*VAR-yohs*
vegetable	legumbre (m)	*leh-GOOM-breh*

Venezuela	Venezuela	*veh-neh-SWEH-la*
Venezuelan	venezolano	*veh-neh-so-LA-no*
verb	verbo	*VEHR-bo*
very	muy	*mwee*
very well	muy bien	*mwee b'yen*
view	vista	*VEESS-ta*
village	aldea	*ahl-DEH-ah*
vinegar	vinagre (m)	*vee-NA-greh*
violin	violín (m)	*v'yo-LEEN*
visa	visa	*VEE-sa*
visit	visita	*vee-SEE-ta*
(to) visit	visitar	*vee-see-TAR*
vivid	vívido	*VEE-vee-doh*
voice	voz (f)	*vohs*
volcano	volcán (m)	*vohl-KAHN*
voyage	viaje (m)	*V'YA-heh*

W

waist	cintura	*seen-TOO-ra*
(to) wait	esperar	*ess-peh-RAR*
Wait here!	¡Espere aquí!	*¡ess-PEH-reh ah-KEE!*
waiter	camarero, mozo	*ka-ma-REH-ro, MO-so*
waitress	camarera, moza	*ka-ma-REH-ra, MO-sa*
(to) walk	caminar	*ka-mee-NAR*
wall	pared (f)	*pa-RED*

wallet	cartera	*kar-TEH-ra*
(to) want	querer	*keh-REHR*
(I) want	(yo) quiero	*K'YEH-ro*
(you sg.) want	(Ud.) quiere	*K'YEH-reh*
(he, she) wants	(él, ella) quiere	*K'YEH-reh*
(we) want	(nosotros) queremos	*keh-REH-mohs*
(they, you pl.) want	quieren (ellos, ellas, Uds.)	*K'YEH-ren*
Do you want . . . ? (pl.)	¿Quiere Ud . . . ?	*¿K'YEH-reh oo-STED . . . ?*
war	guerra	*GHEH-rra*
warm	caliente	*ka-L'YEN-teh*
was (permanent status)	era	*EH-ra*
was (location or temporary status)	estaba	*ess-TA-ba*
(to) wash	lavar	*lu-VAR*
watch	reloj (m)	*reh-LO*
Watch out!	¡Cuidado!	*¡kwee-DA-doh!*
water	el agua (f)	*el AH-gwa*
water-color	acuarela	*ah-kwa-REH-la*
way (manner)	modo	*MO-doh*
way (road)	camino	*ka-MEE-no*
we	nosotros (m), nosotras (f)	*no-SO-trohs, no-SO-trahs*
weak	débil	*DEH-beel*
(to) wear	llevar	*l'yeh-VAR*

weather	tiempo	*T'YEM-po*
wedding	boda	*BO-da*
Wednesday	miércoles	*M'YER-ko-lehs*
week	semana	*seh-MA-na*
weekend	fin de semana (m)	*feen deh seh-MA-na*
(to) weigh	pesar	*peh-SAR*
weight	peso	*PEH-so*
Welcome!	¡Bienvenido!	*¡b'yen-veh-NEE-do!*
You are welcome.	De nada.	*deh NA-da.*
well (adv.)	bien	*b'yen.*
well (water, oil)	pozo	*PO-so*
went		
(I) went	(yo) fui	*fwee*
(he, she, you sg.) went	(él, ella, Ud.) fue	*fweh*
(we) went	(nosotros) fuimos	*FWEE-mohs*
(they, you p.) went	(ellos, ellas, Uds.) fueron	*FWEH-rohn*
were (permanent status)		
(you sg.) were	(Ud.) era	*EH-ra*
(we) were	(nosotros) éramos	*EH-ra-mohs*
(they, you pl.) were	(ellos, ellas, Uds.) eran	*EH-rahn*
were (location or temporary status)		
(you sg.) were	(Ud.) estaba	*ess-TA-ba*
(we) were	(nosotros) estábamos	*ess-TA-ba-mohs*

(they, you pl.) were	(ellos, ellas Uds.) estaban	*ess-TA-bahn*
west	oeste	*oh-ESS-teh*
what	que	*keh*
What's the matter?	¿Qué pasa?	*¿keh PA-sa?*
What time is it?	¿Qué hora es?	*¿keh OH-ra ess?*
What do you want?	¿Qué quiere Ud.?	*¿keh K'YEH-reh oo-STED?*
wheel	rueda	*RWEH-da*
when	cuando	*KWAHN-doh*
where	donde	*DOHN-deh*
wherever	dondequiera	*dohn-deh-K'YEH-ra*
Where to?	¿A dónde?	*ah DOHN-deh?*
whether	si	*see*
which	cual	*kwahl*
while	mientras	*M'YEN-trahs*
white	blanco	*BLAHN-ko*
who	quien	*k'yen*
whole	entero	*en-TEH-ro*
Whom?	¿A quién?	*¿ah k'yen?*
Why?	¿Por qué?	*¿por keh?*
Why not?	¿por qué no?	*¿por keh no?*
wide	ancho	*AHN-cho*
widow	viuda	*V'YOO-da*
widower	viudo	*V'YOO-doh*
wife	esposa	*ess-PO-sa*
wild	salvaje	*sahl-VA-heh*

will

The future is formed by adding one of the following endings to the infinitive of the verb, according to the subject: **(yo) -é (tú) -ás, (él, ella, Ud.) -á, (nosotros) -emos, (ellos, ellas, Uds.) -án.**

I will speak	hablaré	*ah-bla-REH*
they won't speak	no hablarán	*no ah-bla-RAHN*
(to) win	ganar	*ga-NAR*
wind	viento	*V'YEN-toh*
window	ventana	*ven-TA-na*
wine	vino	*VEE-no*
winter	invierno	*een-V'YEHR-no*
(to) wish	desear	*deh-seh-AR*
without	sin	*seen*
wolf	lobo	*LO-bo*
woman	mujer	*moo-HEHR*
wonderful	maravilloso	*ma-ra-veel-YO-so*
won't (See "will.")		
wood	madera	*ma-DEH-ra*
woods	bosque (m)	*BOHS-keh*
wool	lana	*LA-na*
word	palabra	*pa-LA-bra*
work	trabajo	*tra-BA-ho*
(to) work	trabajar	*tra-ba-HAR*
world	mundo	*MOON-doh*
(to) worry	preocuparse	*pre-oh-koo-PAR-seh*
Don't worry.	No se preocupe.	*no seh pre-oh-KOO-peh*

worse	peor	*peh-OR*

would:

Express the idea of "would" by adding the appropriate ending to the infinitive of the verb, according to the subject: **(yo) -ía, (tú) -ías, (el, ella, Ud.) -ía, (nosotros) -íamos, (ellos, ellas, Uds.) -ían.**

I would speak	(yo) hablaría	*ah-bla-REE-ya*
I would learn	(yo) aprendería	*ah-pren-deh-REE-ya*
I would like . . .	Me gustaría . . .	*mch goos-ta-REE-ya . . .*
Would you like . . . ?	¿Le gustaría . . . ?	*¿leh goos-ta-REE-ya . . . ?*
wrist	muñeca	*moon-YEH-ka*
(to) write	escribir	*ess-kree-BEER*
Write it.	Escríbalo.	*ess-KREE-ba-lo.*
writer	escritor	*ess-kree-TOR*
wrong	equivocado	*eh-kee-vo-KA-doh*

Y

year	año	*AHN-yo*
yellow	amarillo	*ah-ma-REEL-yo*
yes	sí	*see*
yesterday	ayer	*ah-YEHR*
yet	todavía	*to-da-VEE-ya*
you	usted (sg.), ustedes (pl.) tú (fam.)	*oo-STED oo-STED-ehs*
young	joven	*HO-ven*
your	su	*soo*

| **yours** | el suyo, la suya | *el SOO-yo, la SOO-ya* |
| **yourself, your-** selves (reflex.) | se | *seh* |

Z

zipper	cierre (m)	*S'YEH-rreh*
zone	zona	*SO-na*
zoo	zoológico	*so-oh-LO-hee-ko*

POINT TO THE ANSWER

For speedy reference and when in doubt, to get a clear answer to a question you have just asked, show the following Spanish pages to the person you are addressing and let him or her point to the answer to your question among the possible answers on these four pages. The sentence in Spanish after the arrow asks the person to point to the answer.

> *Tenga la bondad de indicar en las páginas*
> *siguientes su contestación a mi pregunta.*
> *Muchísimas gracias.*

Sí.
Yes.

No.
No.

Quizás.
Perhaps.

Ciertamente.
Certainly.

Está bien.
All right.

Perdón.
Excuse me.

Comprendo.
I understand.

No comprendo.
I don't understand.

¿Qué desea? **Yo sé.** **No sé.**
What do you I know. I don't know.
want?

Otra vez. **Es bastante.**
Again (or more). Enough.

Abierto. **Cerrado.**
Open. Closed.

Demasiado. **No es suficiente.**
Too much. Not enough.

Prohibido entrar. **Prohibido.**
No admittance. It is forbidden.

Propiedad privada. **Ud. debe irse.**
Private property. You must leave.

Ahora. **Más tarde.** **Demasiado temprano.**
Now. Later. Too early.

Demasiado tarde. **Hoy.** **Mañana.** **Ayer.**
Too late. Today. Tomorrow. Yesterday.

Esta noche. **Anoche.** **Mañana por la**
Tonight. Last night. **noche.**
Tomorrow night.

Esta semana. **La semana** **La semana que**
This week. **pasada.** **viene.**
Last week. Next week.

Es posible. **No es posible.** **De acuerdo.**
It's posible. It's not possible. It is agreed.

Muy bien. **No está bien.** **Es cerca.** **Demasiado**
Very good. It isn't good. It's near. **lejos.**
Too far.

Muy lejos. **Aquí.** **Allá.**
Very far. Here. There.

Doble a la izquierda. **Doble a la derecha.**
Turn left. Turn right.

Siga derecho. **Venga conmigo.** **Sígame.**
Go straight ahead. Come with me. Follow me.

Vamos. **Hemos llegado.** **Pare aquí.**
Let's go. We have arrived. Stop here.

Espéreme. **No puedo.** **Esperaré.**
Wait for me. I cannot. I will wait.

Debo irme. **Regrese más tarde.**
I must go. Come back later.

Regreso en seguida.
I'll be right back.

Él no está aquí. **Ella no está aquí.**
He is not here. She is not here.

Mi nombre es _____. **¿Su nombre?**
Ny name is _____. Your name?

¿Número de teléfono? **¿Dirección?**
Telephone number? Address?

lunes **martes** **miércoles** **jueves**
Monday Tuesday Wednesday Thursday

viernes **sábado** **domingo**
Friday Saturday Sunday

A las _____.
At _____ o'clock.

Cuesta _____ pesos _____ centavos.
It costs _____ pesos _____ centavos.

uno	**dos**	**tres**	**cuatro**	**cinco**
one	two	three	four	five

seis	**siete**	**ocho**	**nueve**	**diez**
six	seven	eight	nine	ten

once	**doce**	**trece**	**catorce**	**quince**
eleven	twelve	thirteen	fourteen	fifteen

dieciséis	**diecisiete**	**dieciocho**
sixteen	seventeen	eighteen

diecinueve	**veinte**	**treinta**
nineteen	twenty	thirty

cuarenta	**cincuenta**	**sesenta**
forty	fifty	sixty

setenta	**ochenta**	**noventa**
seventy	eighty	ninety

cien	**mil**	**diez mil**
one hundred	one thousand	ten thousand